The Out of Doors Club

Four of the Band

THE OUT OF
DOORS CLUB

SAMUEL SCOVILLE Jr.

Republished by the
South Jersey Culture & History Center, 2018

*This edition published 2018
by the South Jersey Culture & History Center*

*South Jersey Culture & History Center,
Stockton University,
101 Vera King Farris Drive
Galloway, New Jersey 08205*

*Title: The Out of Doors Club
Author: Samuel Scoville Jr.*

For Mother and Trottie and Honey and Henny Penny and Alice Palace and the dear Third who waits Beyond for the rest of the band, this little Book of their Deeds and Darings is written

—by—
THE CAPTAIN

This is the story of five children and a father and a mother who found their way into a new world. The way is open to all children and to all fathers and mothers, and good friends and happy adventures await them there.

SAMUEL SCOVILLE JR.
Philadelphia

CONTENTS

FOREWORD

Samuel Scoville Jr.'s *The Out of Doors Club*, published in 1919, expertly blends the genres of biography, nature writing and fiction, presenting twenty brief essays that achieve striking realism as they weave together personal memories, real and imagined. The collection—perhaps novel is a better descriptor—records Scoville's adventures in nature accompanied by his five young children, affectionately named the "Band." Most, if not all, of these adventures take place in the Pine Barrens of New Jersey.

Scoville (1872–1950) was a storyteller. He was also an attorney, writer, public speaker, out-door enthusiast and, if the stories in this volume are to be believed, a devoted and loving father. Born in Norwich, New York, he was the grandson of the well-known nineteenth-century religious leader Henry Ward Beecher. He attended and graduated from Yale University (1889–1893), where he was noted for his athleticism. Two years later, he received a law degree from the University of the State of

New York. He married Katharine Gallaudet Trumbull of Philadelphia in 1899, and soon after they started their family. Throughout his life, Scoville exhibited great passion for the outdoors and was a longtime member of the Delaware Valley Ornithological Club, one of the nation's oldest birding organizations. He chronicled his frequent trips into the field in numerous articles and books.

In this volume, Scoville concentrates on jaunts taken with his children, the Band. From oldest to youngest, the Band is comprised of his five nicknamed children: the Third, Trottie, Honey, Henny-Penny and Alice-Place. The last two are regularly described as twins, and here the stories wander into a fictive reality. Scoville's youngest child, and only daughter, Alice, was born in 1911. She is clearly identifiable as Alice-Palace. Her twin in the stories, Henny-Penny, corresponds to the real-life Henry Ward Beecher Scoville, but he was born two years earlier in 1909. Honey is identifiable as William Beecher Scoville, born in 1906; and Trottie is Gurdon Trumbull Beecher, born in 1904.

Understanding the real-life fate of Samuel Scoville 3rd, the fictitious Third, deepens one's appreciation for the goals and achievements of this work. Scoville deftly draws the character of each child, but the Third is perhaps the least identifiable: he is simply the oldest and always competent, little more. Born in 1902, Samuel Scoville 3rd was indeed the eldest child of the family, but he died at two years of age, many years before these stories were written. In the dedication to this volume Scoville describes him as "the dear Third who waits Beyond for the rest of the Band." It becomes clear that Scoville is recreating the family that might have been, touching readers with the emotion he so clearly holds for each of his creations.

The Out of Doors Club allows readers to remember the simpler times in life—when the world held fewer cares and nature walks with father could be the highlight of the day. Trekking through fields, bogs and forests, and canoeing down rivers, the Band learn amusing lessons about nature and life. Readers, meanwhile, appreciate the gentle and loving relationship depicted between father, mother, and children. Throughout, Scoville captures the beautiful innocence and imagination of the young.

This volume has a sister publication. It is the prequel, by one year, to Scoville's *Everyday Adventures*, recently republished by the South Jersey Culture & History Center. We enjoyed that text so much that we turned immediately to republication of *The Out of Doors Club*. If you like one, you will surely like the other.

Gabriela Siwiec
Nathaniel Hartsough
Samantha Wyld
Tom Kinsella

WHO'S WHO IN THE BAND

Samuel Scoville Jr.: "The Captain," "Fathy," "Friar Tuck"
Katharine Gallaudet Trumbull Scoville: "Mothy," "The
   Quarter-Master-General," "The Judge"

Samuel Scoville 3rd (1902–1904): "Third," "Little John"
Gurdon Trumbull Scoville (1904–1993): "Trottie,"
   "Robin Hood"
William Beecher Scoville (1906–1984): "Honey," "Allan
   a'Dale"
Henry Ward Beecher Scoville (1909–1924): "Henny-
   Penny," "Will Scarlet"
Alice Scoville Barry (1911–2012): "Alice-Palace," "Maid
   Marion"

FREE LUNCH

The Out of Doors Club, known as the Band for short, was a secret organization which specialized in desperate out of door adventures. It was led by the Captain, who in private life was known as Fathy. The other officers were the Third, Trottie, Honey, Henny-Penny, and Alice-Palace. There were no privates. Then there was Mother, the Quartermaster General, Minnie and Annie in charge of the Commissary, and old John the gardener, the head of the Engineer Corps.

Today when the Band had met for its weekly walk the lunch had been entrusted to Honey. There was a long, dry, spicy saveloy sausage wrapped in tissue paper, a cluster of raisins, three thick scones apiece, and a little package of cocoa, which could be brewed in the tin cup which the Captain carried in a pocket of his khaki shooting jacket. All of these necessary and appetizing articles had been wrapped in a tight little bundle and left on the hall table by long-suffering Minnie, the cook, the night before.

There had been an early breakfast and a five-mile tramp to the frozen depths of Blacksnake Swamp. This great marsh, which was so treacherous and impassable in summer, was today frozen hard and safe, and bottomless Mirror Pool looked like black glass. They explored all of its secret places. Just as they suspected, the Band found that the long-billed marsh-wren nested among the cattails which grew in the very heart of the swamp, guarded in summer by a stretch of quivering, impassable mud. There were the nests, made of the stalks of cattails bent down and thatched on the outside with grass, like big brown balls. Inside, they were lined with soft, velvety down from the heads of the cattails.

There were five nests, but the Captain said that probably they were all the work of one pair of birds. After the nest is built the father marsh wren has a funny habit of building a lot of other nests while the mother wren is sitting. Perhaps he does this to keep himself in practice for another year, or perhaps he thinks that he can fool any one coming to rob the nest by having a lot of false nests around the real one. At any rate, there are usually four or five nests to each marsh wren family.

Over beyond the cattails was a wide grassy stretch, covered smooth with white snow. There the Band did some trailing and tracking.

They found innumerable rabbit tracks, two holes wide apart and two holes close together; and the Captain said the rabbit was going in the direction of the wide apart marks. He explained that every time Bunny jumped his long hind legs came out in front, and made the far apart marks, while the two little fore legs made the other marks which were close together.

Everywhere, too, there was a tracery of fine, delicate little paw prints with the marks of long tails. These were made by the meadow mice, which tunnel under the snow, and are just as active in winter as in summer.

Among them was a strange track, almost like the trail of a snake; only, of course, all the snakes were fast asleep far underground. It was a wide trough, with little, close-set, zigzag paw marks all through it. The Captain told the Band that this was the trail of the fierce blarina shrew, one of the greatest killers known.

"If the blarina were as large as a dog," said the Captain, "we should not be safe anywhere, for every one of them eats twice its own weight in flesh every twenty-four hours. Under ground, above ground, or under the water it kills and kills and kills. It has to," went on the Captain, "for it starves to death in six hours if it can't get flesh."

The Band regarded the strange tracks with enormous interest.

"How big do they grow?" anxiously inquired Henny-Penny, the littlest but one of the Band.

"Just about as long as my middle finger," the Captain reassured him. Suddenly in the midst of all of these snow stories the Band began to get hungry.

"Lunchtime!" they all shouted together.

Then it was that the guilty Honey remembered for the first time that the lunch was lying on the hall table instead of bulging out of his pocket. There was great wrath among the other members of the Band when he faltered out the sad truth.

"Five miles from home, and our whole day spoiled," wailed Trottie, always the hungriest of them all. Even Henny-Penny, usually Honey's firmest ally, regarded him reproachfully, while Alice-Palace, the littlest of the Band, lifted up her voice several feet in an exhibition of grief that bade fair to scare away even the bloodthirsty blarinas for miles around. Only quick action on the part of the Captain saved the day.

"Comrades," said he, placing one hand over Alice-Palace' s widely opened mouth, "all is not lost. Woodsmen like ourselves can find food anywhere. Follow me. Hist!"

Like Hawkeye and Chingachguch and other well-known scouts, the Captain always employed that mysterious word when beginning a desperate adventure. The Band followed him to the other side of the great swamp. They crossed a brook, and found themselves in a little grove of swamp-maples which had grown around the fallen trunk of the parent tree. The Captain scanned the snow carefully. Everywhere were trails which, like rabbit tracks, by their position showed that they had been made by some animal which hopped. Instead of the holes made by the rabbits there were little pawmarks, and the Captain told the Band that these were the tracks of gray squirrels, which had come down through the woods into the marsh.

"Cheer up, comrades," he said, looking carefully among the trees; "I see something."

Even as he spoke, he reached up; and there, wedged in between a little twig and the smooth trunk of a swamp-maple sapling, was a big, dry, seasoned black walnut. Then the Band began to look, and they found the leafless trees filled with walnuts, each one wedged so that it would not blow down.

Up and about the low trees climbed and scrambled the Band. It was great fun. Sometimes the nuts were hidden and sometimes in plain sight, but all together there was nearly half a peck of them, seasoned until the rich gold kernel was dry and crisp. They had come upon the winter storehouse of a gray-squirrel family. The red squirrel, as the Captain explained to them, hides his nuts in heaps in hollow trees or under rocks, but the gray squirrel tucks his away separately one by one. When at last the nuts had been collected, they were all piled together in the lee of a big black Oak tree where the campfire was to be made. When this was done, the Band were anxious to qualify as expert nut crackers, but the Captain would not let them begin.

"We've got to get our dessert before we start lunch," he said, leading them back into the swamp.

Beside a broken-down rail fence he stopped, before a thicket of tiny trees with smooth trunks, whose gray twigs were loaded down with bunches of what looked like little purple plums. Each one had a layer of dried blue sweet pulp over a flat stone; and the pulp, what there was of it, was as sweet as sugar, with a curious spicy taste. The Captain told them that these were nannie plums, belonging to the viburnum family.

Farther on they found clusters of little purple fox grapes, fiercely sour in the fall, but under the bite of the frost they had sweetened enough to be swallowed.

Still the Captain was not ready to sit down. Up the hillside he led them, by a winding path through tangled thickets, until in a level place beside a little brook he brought them to a group of curious trees. The bark of these was deeply grooved and in places nearly three inches thick. The stiff branches were covered with scores of golden-red globes. Some were wrinkled and frost bitten until they had turned brown, but others still hung plump and bright in the winter air. It was a persimmon grove which the Captain had discovered.

Before he could be stopped Henny-Penny had picked one of the best looking of the lot, and took a deep bite of the soft, luscious fruit. Immediately thereafter he spat out his first taste of persimmon with great emphasis, his mouth so puckered that it was with difficulty that he could express his entirely unfavorable opinion of the new fruit.

"Handsome is as handsome does," warned the Captain. "Try some of the frost-bitten ones."

Accordingly the Band selected the worst-looking specimens they could find on the trees, and found that the more wrinkled the persimmon, the sweeter the taste and the less the pucker.

On the way back the Captain suddenly stopped. In front of him grew several small trees whose branches were all matted together here and there in tangled bunches which looked like birds' nests. At the end of the twigs grew single round purple berries about the size of a wild cherry. Alice-Palace said this must be the bird's-nest tree, but the Captain told them that these were young hackberry trees. They picked handfuls of these berries, which had a sweet, spicy pulp over a fragile stone that could be crushed like the seeds of a raisin. In fact, the berry very much resembled the raisin in taste.

The camp once reached, there followed a feast which the Band never forgot. Around a roaring fire of dry hickory and sassafras branches they sat with their backs against the great oak tree, and cracked and cracked and cracked nuts, which tasted far better than any tame ones which could be bought at grocery stores. Along with the nuts they crunched sugar berries, and nibbled nannie plums, and tasted frost grapes, while for dessert each one had a handful of the honey-sweet wrinkled persimmons. "It was lucky for Honey, though," said Trottie, "that the Captain was along. If we hadn't found this lunch, we'd have left him tied to a tree for the blarinas to eat up."

THE SEVEN SLEEPERS

"Safe from sorrow and sin and death," read Mother as she finished the legend of the Saints at Ephesus, "the Seven sleep sweet in that cave until Christ cometh again."

The Band was spending two winter days and nights at the Cabin.

"I wisht, I wisht," said Alice-Palace at last, "that I could see the nice dear Sleepers."

"Well," said the Captain from the depths of a monstrous rocking chair, "there are seven other sleepers who live not far from this Cabin, but they aren't saints by any means. Some are gentle and some are fierce."

"Tell us," chorused the Band from in front of the fire that roared in the great arched fireplace.

"The first one," said the Captain, "is big and black and dangerous."

"Bumbly-bee!" shouted Alice-Palace. "That's big an' black an' very dangerous," she explained, "cause once I caught one an' he hurt me norful." "No," said the Captain, "this is a big, black, growly animal who wears an overcoat of four inches of fur and an undercoat of four inches of fat. He isn't afraid of the cold, but he finds that rent is cheaper than board. So he sleeps all winter instead of eating."

"Bear," shouted all but one of the Band. "Bumbly-bee," piped Alice-Palace, who was never known to change an opinion.

"Once," said the Captain, "I knew two boys—one was twelve and the other was ten years old. They went off hunting up in Maine in March. One had a muzzle-loading shotgun and the other had a long stick. They found a little hole in a bank," he went on, "and the boy with the stick poked. He felt something soft, so he kept on poking. 'I think there's something here,' he said. There was. All of a sudden the whole bank caved in and out rushed a big, black, cross bear. You see," explained the Captain, "they had poked right into the air hole of a bear-den. The snow was so deep that they couldn't run, and the bear could climb a tree much faster than they could. So what do you suppose they did?"

"I guess," remarked Alice resentfully, "that they wisht it had been a bumbly-bee."

"Go on!" shouted the rest with one accord.

"The little chap with the stick," continued the Captain, "got behind the big one with the gun, who was shaking like anything. 'Don't you miss,' he said, cause this stick isn't very sharp.' 'All right,' said the big boy, and he waited until he saw the white spot that showed under the bear's chin when it reared up on its hind legs not six feet away. The shot crashed right through the bear's throat, and he fell dead so close to their feet that the hot blood stained the shoes of the boy in front. They got ten dollars for the skin, and ten dollars bounty, and about three million dollars of glory."

"Tell some more," chorused the Band when he stopped for breath.

"Well," meditated the Captain, "there was my great, great Uncle Jake who fought in the Revolution and was a famous bear hunter. One day during a January thaw he was coming down Pond Hill when he stepped into a mushy place back of a patch of bushes and sank in up to his waist. He felt something soft under his feet, and he stamped on it. The next second," said the Captain impressively, "he wished he hadn't, for a big animal rose right up under him, and the next thing poor Uncle Jake knew he was astride a bear going downhill like mad, riding bear back as it were."

Mother gave a deep groan and buried her face in her hands; but the rest of the Band were too young to be affected by the pun.

"He didn't want to stay on, and he didn't dare to get off," resumed the Captain hurriedly, "so he drew his hunting knife and waited until the old bear reached level ground and just stabbed him dead right through his neck."

"Tell us about some more," urged Trottie when the Captain stopped again.

"Some of the gently ones," suggested Henny-Penny, beginning to look around anxiously at the dark corners.

"Well," said the Captain, "there's a gray, greedy one who goes to bed early, just a loose bag of fat. That's the woodchuck. Then there's a nice striped one with pockets in his cheeks, who always takes a quart or so of nuts and seeds to bed with him in case he gets hungry in the night. That's the chipmunk."

"Nice dear Chippy Nipmunk," explained Alice-Palace to the Third.

"Then comes a chap with a funny face and a ringed tail and whose hind paws make a track like a baby's foot. That's the raccoon. The next one is pretty dangerous," continued the Captain. "He is black and white and has a long bushy tail. He won't turn out of his way for anybody, but he'll always give any one that comes up to him three signals before he defends himself. First," said the Captain, "he'll stamp his forefeet. Second, he'll raise his long bushy tail. If you still keep on coming he gives his third and last signal. He waves the end of his tail back and forth. If you stand still," finished the Captain impressively, "or move backward, you are safe even then, but if you take one step forward—you'll have to buy a new suit of clothes."

"I know," remarked the Third wisely, "Bill Darby and I caught one in a trap once. He said it was an albino woodchuck. But it was a skunk an' we had to live in our bathing suits for nearly a week.

"The next sleeper," said the Captain, "has wings."

"A bumbly-bee," tried Alice again. "No," returned the Captain patiently, "this is an animal with a very ugly face and leathery brown wings with hooks on the top.

When it goes to sleep for the winter it catches these little hooks on a rafter or beam in some dark corner of a building or steeple. Then it turns and hangs by the long curved nails of its hind feet and goes to sleep upside down. It makes a very high squeak when it flies, and sometimes it comes into houses hunting mosquitoes. It never does any harm, and it does a great deal of good; but silly people," went on the Captain severely, looking straight at Trottie, "sometimes kill them with tennis rackets."

"I won't kill any more bats," murmured Trottie penitently.

"Last of all," resumed the Captain, "is the dear little jumping mouse. He has big eyes and floppy ears and a long, long tail. If you boys could jump as far in proportion to your height as Mr. Jumping Mouse does, you would clear two hundred and forty feet every time you jumped. Before the frost comes he makes a round warm nest of leaves and soft grass, far underground. There he rolls himself into a round ball and sleeps until spring."

"I like the cuddly jumpy-mouse the best," said Alice-Palace sleepily.

Then Mother announced that it was bedtime for seven other sleepers.

"Just one minute," said the Captain. "I want to read the Band a very, very beautiful poem which has the names of the seven animals that sleep all winter, so that the Band can remember them. I know it's a beautiful poem," he finished modestly, "because I wrote it myself.

"Here is the poem:

The Bat and the Bear they never care
What winter winds may blow,
The Jumping Mouse in his cosy house
Is safe from ice and snow.
The Chipmunk and the Woodchuck,
The Skunk who's slow but sure.
The ringed Raccoon, who hates the moon,
Have found for cold the cure."

THE DAY OF THE WINTER TURTLE

All out for the Cranberry Country," shouted the Captain up the staircase. It was so early on a Saturday morning that the winter sky was just beginning to redden in the east. Then he whistled the red bird note, the adventure call of the Band. Followed the instantaneous thump of Trottie's bare feet on the floor, an answering whistle from Henny-Penny that sounded like a small steam siren, a squeal from Alice-Palace's room, a shout from the Third, and last a long yawn from the unhurrying Honey. The Band was aroused.

"Skates and sweaters," were the marching orders. There was the sound of hasty splashings and brushings and scrubbings from the upper bathrooms. Twenty minutes later the Band was met around the breakfast table.

"Don't you go to the office today, Fathy?" inquired the thoughtful Third. He was nicknamed the Third because he had the same name as the Captain and the Captain's father, whom they all called Pater.

"When the bogs are frozen,
    And the weather's fine,
No indoor work
    For me or mine!"

loudly declaimed the Captain with wonderful gestures, like Trottie speaking a piece on a Friday afternoon.

"I made up that beautiful poem," he announced when the Band had stopped laughing. "Moreover, that's the law, and I wouldn't dare break it."

"I guess you made up that law, too," said Mother, who was always pretending to scold the Captain because he left his law office so often to take trips with the Band.

"Well, it's a good law, anyway," returned the Captain, taking a long breath. "All those in favor of it make a loud noise."

If there had sounded one more vote in the affirmative, the windows would undoubtedly have been blown out. As it was, Minnie the cook came rushing in with a dipper of water, under the impression that her favorite fear of a fire had at last come to pass; and Mother said, when she took her hands off her ears, that she was deaf for life. The Captain, however, who had made the loudest noise of all, announced that the Holiday Bill was carried by a very close vote.

Two hours later found the whole Band in a new country. Underfoot was snowy sand. Overhead were low pines whose stiff needles came in clusters of threes, and cedars with rounded instead of pointed leaves. The Captain told them that the pines were the pitch pines instead of the white pines to which they were accustomed, and that the cedars were white instead of red cedars. Then there were thickets of little oak trees not more than three feet high, with three cornered leaves with a little thorn at each corner, and others with ridged bark and leaves that looked like chestnut leaves. The first of these, he said, were the scrub oak, and every tree in spite of its size was a full grown tree, perhaps many years old; while the other was the chestnut-leaved oak.

Another tree the Third, who was a boy scout, said was a black oak. He told by cutting a piece out of the bark with his bowie knife (it was really a jackknife, but the Third always spoke of it as a bowie). The inner bark showed bright yellow, and the Third said that was the sign of a black oak. Alice-Palace said it ought to have been black, and that for her part she intended to call the tree the yellow oak. There was quite an argument until the Captain said that the Third was right, and showed them also a white oak which had a whitish gray bark. Then beside a brook they found a plant that looked like a vine climbing up a bush. Its leaves were of a fresh green, untouched by the frost, and grew on a stiff, brittle stem that looked as if it were fine-drawn copper wire. The leaves themselves were like flat green hands, each with three, four, or five fingers and a thumb. They were beautifully marked with a pattern of fine lines, and both the texture and the color were different on the underside.

The Captain told them that the plant was the rare climbing fern, which like the Christmas fern keeps green all winter.

Finally the Bog was reached, a sheet of ice like black glass. Around it ran dykes, which when crossed showed a chain of other bogs that stretched for miles through the woods. It was wonderful skating. In and out among the trees they went, following ditches through mile-long marshes, circling ringing little pools that gleamed like mirrors made of green jade, and gliding cautiously over treacherous places where the warm, yellow-green sphagnum moss had made the ice soft.

After a while they all cut hockey sticks, and the Captain taught them how to make perfect ones by bending down saplings and building a fire underneath the bent part, which straightway thereafter stayed bent. Then they played "keep away" with an old doorknob for a puck, which, providentially, was found in Henny-Penny's pocket, along with about four pounds of other bric-a-brac. Then came hill-dill and cross tag.

But, after all, the best fun was the Speedway Fast Freight. The Captain would start first, and behind him all the Band would be strung out holding on to each other's hockey sticks in a line. The train would whiz down the long level ditches, whirl squealingly around sharp corners and in and out among the bushes and trees, losing a car now and then when the turns were too sharp or the speed too great. It was by one of these accidents that Alice-Palace made a great scientific discovery. She had been the little caboose, which is always found at the end of all well-regulated freight trains. When the fast train zipped in and out among some patches of dangleberry bushes at the far end of the marsh, the coupling broke, or the brakes locked, or there was a hot box, or some other railroad calamity occurred. At any rate the wheels of the little caboose left the tracks, and she overturned with a startling bump as the train disappeared around the corner.

There was a piercing shriek of distress, and the Fast Freight came to a standstill and was hastily organized into a wrecking train which back tracked its way to the accident. As they came within sight of the wreck they noted that the little caboose lay prostrate, face downward, on the clear ice. The Captain shot away from the rest of the Band as if they were anchored—for under the martial sternness necessary to control the desperate characters who followed his fortunes, the Captain concealed a certain amount of affection for the youngest of the Band.

"What's the matter, Alice?" he called anxiously as she still lay face downward even when he reached her.

"Turties," responded Alice muffledly, with her mouth close to the ice.

"What?" questioned the Captain bewilderedly.

"Turties, nice crawly turties, two of 'em," repeated Alice, pointing a mittened forefinger downward.

Sure enough, before the delighted eyes of the whole Band there they were! Two turtles about the size of the Captain's hand were moving with quick strokes under the clear ice here and there, in plain sight through little thickets of golden green water-weed. It was a delight to watch the swift, effortless way in which they moved, so different from the painstaking progress of a turtle on land. At each alternate stroke the little legs, armed with long curved claws, would float loose without any resistance to the water until in position again for another stroke.

"Just as if they were swimming the 'crawl,'" said the Third.

"They are," said the Captain, "they invented it."

The backs of both swimmers were olive-black in color. Around the edge of the upper shell was a loud pattern of yellow bordered vermilion shields and bars and crescents, while their heads were striped with bright yellow, and their necks with yellow and red.

"They look all painted," remarked Henny-Penny, nearly freezing his little nose against the ice.

"That's their name, 'Painted Turtle,'" said the Captain, "only they're really terrapin, and they belong to the same family as the diamond-backed terrapin, which is worth its weight in silver."

"Terrapin," he explained, "are freshwater turtles which are good to eat."

For a long time the Band watched them swim around. Not a look did the turtles give to their audience, even when they rapped hard on the ice above them.

"I always thought until today," soliloquized the Captain, "and all the books say, that turtles hibernate in winter under the mud like water snakes and frogs."

It was Henny-Penny who put an end to this research work.

"It's lunchtime by my tummy."

"Mine too," shouted the rest of the Band.

"Your tummies are fast," objected the Captain, "it's only half past eleven."

His watch, however, was unanimously overruled by the more accurate timekeepers, and in a few moments the whole Band was on the bank of one of the bogs. A long dry log made a good seat. In front was a dead stump. Against this the fire was built so that its hollow side would reflect the heat. My, how good everything did taste! Never were there such chops and such delicious strips of bacon as the Captain drew out of one of the pockets of his shooting jacket, all wrapped up in tissue paper. These the Band roasted on long sharp sticks. And when he drew out packages of cluster raisins, and handfuls of nuts, which the Band cracked lingeringly on the log with round pebbles, the lunch became a feast. The winter sun was westering well down the sky when the Band finally started back, and the stars were out when they reached home, and Mother, and—supper.

THE STORMING OF FORT HILL

It was snowing hard, and the Band stared sadly out of the windows. They had planned to celebrate Washington's Birthday by skating. Now the skating was spoiled and, worst of all, the Captain had not come home from the office, as he had hoped to do. It looked like a wasted holiday. Suddenly from the white swirl sounded the call of the cardinal grosbeak.

"It's the Captain," shouted Trottie and the Third.

"It's Fathy," squealed Honey and Henny-Penny and Alice-Palace.

Sure enough, in another minute the Captain came stamping in, covered with snow.

"Comrades," he said impressively, winding a bandanna around his neck, "we attack Fort Hill at sunset. If there be any here who for the sake of their wives and families wish to draw back, now is the time."

"I haven't got any wife," piped up Henny-Penny, "nor any family 'cept this one. But I want to come."

The rest of the Band followed his lead. Not one of them drew back. The Captain said it made the blood run faster in his shriveled old veins to have such gallant comrades.

"To horse," he shouted a minute later, grabbing a six-foot sled and shooting off across the icy lawn. The rest of the Band followed him whoopingly on sleds of all sizes and colors. Down the slope they sped into the winding driveway, and followed its turns until they shot one after another out of the stone gate and stopped in the sunken lane which ran past Wentworth Farm. As they plodded through the stinging snow, a bird dived into a patch of bushes directly ahead.

"A cardinal," said Trottie, the bird expert, "I saw the color."

The rest of the Band doubted, but a few steps farther on and they all saw his blood-red crest against the white and green of a snow-covered cedar and heard his loud whistle. Farther on a little gray and black bird flitted along the roadside, which even Alice-Palace recognized by the flash of its snowy white tail-feathers.

"It's a bunco," she called out loudly.

"Junco, you mean," said her twin, Henny-Penny, and there followed an argument which lasted until they reached old Tory Bridge. One of Washington's scouts had once hidden under it when pursued by a Tory troop, gripping his horse's muzzle firmly lest it should neigh as the enemy's horsemen thundered above him. Beyond the bridge a flock of purple black birds flew up with creaking calls from the neighboring meadow, circled once among the snowflakes, and disappeared over the next hill.

"Purple grackles," shouted Trottie and the Third.

"Purply crackles," piped up Alice-Palace after the rest,—"cause they make a crackling noise," she explained.

"It's a record," said Trottie. "We got them on March first last year." And down went the crackling grackles on the year's bird list.

At the very crest of the hill the Captain halted the Band. To the left a long meadow sloped away to the valley below, almost lost to sight in the snow flurries. Without a word the Captain climbed the ice-covered rail fence, dragging his long sled behind him, followed by the Band.

"Beyond that oak-tree down the meadow is Fort Hill," he said. "No one has ever tried coasting down it. Comrades Henry and Alice are to stop at the tree, and Trottie and Honey are not to do any racing. Follow me," he finished, "and don't fall off." The sleds sped through the frozen grass and ice-covered weeds, which snapped and broke and tinkled like glass. Gradually the pace became swifter. Just beyond the oak tree the Captain, who was leading, disappeared over the edge of what seemed to his startled eyes a precipice. Then he struck a pile of snow covered cornstalks and sailed out into the air. He clung to his spirited steed with a death grip and struck ground again some ten yards further on with a grunt.

By this time his sled, although ordinarily well broken, was excited beyond control. It shot down the icy hill with a crash that sounded like a bullet going through a dozen windowpanes. The sharp fragments from the ice-covered grass cut into the Captain's face like hail. In an instant with one last flying leap his sled was speeding like a bullet across the flat toward a stone wall. It was impossible to turn the bolting sled on the ice without skidding. Suddenly, just as the wall loomed up dead ahead, the sled struck a stretch of drifted snow, and the Captain made a sharp curve and came to a stop just in time to watch the rest of the Band take the hill.

First came the Third. He leaped over the edge like a startled chamois, with a loud squeal when he saw what was in front of him. The pile of cornstalks he missed by a hair's breadth. Gaining control of his sled far more quickly than his leader had done, he went whizzing safely by, kicking his legs insultingly in the air as he passed.

Then came Trottie and Honey, disobediently racing as usual. They had been running into each other and jockeying for position all the way down the meadow. All bickerings stopped at the edge of the precipice.

"Gee!" they both howled in terror as they shot out into the atmosphere. Honey followed the Third's safe track. Trottie, however, struck the cornstalk pile full and fair. He seemed to Honey to soar into the air like a swallow, and then went whizzing down the descent. As he saw the stone wall in front he gave a terrified yell, but just then he struck the saving stretch of soft snow, and amid a spindrift of frozen flakes whirled gaspingly to where the Captain's craft lay at anchor.

Then two little round heads peered over the edge of the slope. They belonged to Alice-Palace and Henny-Penny, who had obediently stopped at the oak tree.

"There's a littly weeny bird up here," Alice shrieked down to them. Through the flakes flew a tiny bird.

"See-see-see," it called in a tiny, high-pitched note.

"Golden crowned kinglet!" shouted Trottie exultingly, and so it was.

Slowly they climbed the long slope down which they had flashed a few minutes before. As they reached the top of the hill, suddenly the sky all around them grew pink, the snowflakes stopped falling, and in the west gleamed a heart of glowing, shifting flame. The sky to each side brightened into pale gold. The silver bars of the ice-covered branches could not keep back the glory that streamed from the sunset. The caw of a passing crow came down from the cold sky and against the afterglow they saw a sparrow hawk perched on his watchtower.

Up the slope the Captain dragged the two littlest members of the Band. Then they all got on their sleds and pretended that it was three hundred years ago, when wolves were everywhere. As they sped down the road, they could almost hear the pattering of swift feet and see galloping forms black against the snow. Down the last hill they rushed and whizzed in at the home gate. Across the lawn shone the yellow lamplight of home. Five minutes later the whole Band rushed in the door and all together told Mother of the day's doings.

THE FEN FOLK

The Band was abroad again, and this time in a far country. Only the Captain knew the paths and the dwellers in this lone marshland. First they crossed a great river where from the ferryboat they saw their first herring gulls. The snow-white ones with black tips to their wings, the Captain said, were the grown-ups, while the smoky gray and black drab birds were the little-ups. On the New Jersey side they followed a winding road through the woods, and on the way they learned many new evergreens. One was a tree with red berries and stiff, bright green thorny leaves.

"I don't know the name of it," said Trottie, pricking his nose severely, trying to smell the berries, "but they are the same leaves that Mother buys for Christmas greens every year."

"Quite right," said the Captain, "it's holly, and if we could make it grow over on our side of the river she wouldn't have to buy any more."

Then he showed them the little fatal sheep laurel with its green, drooping leaves, which kill sheep when they nibble them in winter; dark green glossy leaves of the mountain laurel, whose dead branches make wonderful firewood; and the wider, smooth, drooping green leaves of the wild sweet magnolia, whose gray bark is spicy like the spice-bush or the sassafras, yet with a gingery bite of its own. Then there were the climbing fern, and the wintergreen leaves which the Band ate by handfuls, to say nothing of white cedars, and pitch-pines with their needles in clusters of threes, and the yellow pines whose needles were usually arranged in twos. The last of the evergreens was a bush with olive-green leaves and tiny, bitter, black berries. It was the ink berry, a poor relation of the Christmas holly, for in spite of its duller leaves and murky berries it is a holly too.

Near the ink berry was another shrub, with flat, frostbitten, greenish brown leaves and curious wrinkled waxy white berries growing directly from the stem. The Captain picked a few of the leaves, crushed them in his hand, and thrust them under the Third's straight little nose.

"Smells like a barbershop," remarked the latter, and the children all took turns in sniffing the sweet, spicy perfume of the bruised leaves.

"It's the bayberry," explained the Captain; and he told them how his grandmother used to melt the outside waxy flakes of the berries and make wonderful bayberry wax candles, and how one would perfume the little bedroom up under the eaves in which he slept when he went to visit her. The Band picked bunches to take home to Mother, but the Captain said he didn't believe she knew how to make candles.

The air was like iced wine with the perfume of the pines, and in spite of the cold the Band had never seen such a deep blue sky, even in midsummer. On a crooked stream, steeped amber-brown and sweet by millions of cedar roots, stood the Cabin. Inside, the Captain lighted a roaring fire of scrub oak sticks and black oak logs, and they all sat around and toasted their toes while he brewed a great flagon of mulled ale. It smelled a good deal like cocoa, and the flagon looked like a brown pitcher that had once stood in Mother's china closet; but that other gay and gallant Band that had hunted the dun deer in Merry England in the brave days of old had been partial to mulled ale, and what was good enough for Robin Hood was good enough for any one—so argued the Band.

On the way to Indiola Bog, where cranberries were raised on hundreds of acres of lonely, flooded woodland, a tiny bird darted in and out along the roadside like a mouse. It was only in sight a moment, but that was enough for Honey, the Sharp Eyes of the Band.

"It's a little tiny wren," he shouted, "I can see his long curved beak and his funny, perty tail."

"A winter wren," chanted Trottie the ornithologist, who spent all his spare time in poring over bird books, "the fourth smallest bird in the Eastern States, found along brook sides, a winter resident," he quoted. A winter wren it was, and all the Band at once noted it down on their yearly bird sheets, on which was kept a list of birds seen during the year. Alice-Palace had to print the name, and she spelled it "winturren" in spite of Henny-Penny's protest.

"If 'r-e-n' doesn't spell 'wren,' what does it spell?" said Alice-Palace.

For two miles the Band wound its way along a delightfully concealed path, which began at a little door back of Sam Carpenter's sawmill, and crept through the middle of thickets, along the edge of little lakes and across rushing brooks on single logs, but so hidden that strangers would never have found it. For the owners of cranberry bogs set in the middle of the woods were not anxious to have the way to the same at all well known. The Captain, however, knew all the secret paths. He could go to Gum Sprung, where the pitcher plants grew, and knew the way to Ong's Hat, where the hat of that murdered chief had been found a century ago. He could follow the maze of wood roads to Mount Misery, Double Trouble, Apple Pie Hill, Friendship, and all the other little settlements hidden away in the heart of the great pine barrens.

By the time Indiola Bog had been reached the Band was ready for lunch, and immediately scattered to bring in firewood.

"No sticks with bark on," warned the Captain, "it makes a smoke which may betray us to the lurking blood-thirsty Mingoes. Moreover, it's hard on the eyes."

In a surprisingly short time all of the Band were back. Each one had been well drilled in his part of the fire making.

Alice-Palace had brought a double handful of the dryest brown leaves she could find. Henny-Penny picked up nothing except brittle little twigs and stems of dead dry blueberry bushes, which burn furiously and with intense heat.

Honey and Trottie brought in armfuls of dead scrub oak trees, which make a clear hot fire, and sassafras saplings, which burn with a scented flame.

The Third and the Captain staggered in bearing pine stumps which looked like prodigious double teeth with long, resinous roots. These had been grubbed up when the bog was made, and burned with a dull-red, intense glow.

When the wood was all heaped up high to one side the Captain knelt down, and around Alice-Palace's ball of dry leaves built a little tepee of tiny blueberry twigs. Then came the blueberry bushes, and a pile of scrub oak held down by anchors of pine stumps.

Alice-Palace, as the littlest of the Band, was allowed to light the fire. In a moment a stream of smokeless flame shot up, and a few minutes later there was a roaring pillar of fire five feet high.

Then came wassail and feastings galore. Each of the Band broiled a chop cunningly fastened to the end of a long, five-foot oaken broiler. And there were scones and rusks and cookies. The loving cup—it was of the folding variety—was passed from hand to hand, filled high with more mulled ale of the cocoa-brand brewed by the Captain in a little aluminum skillet that he produced from the mysterious depths of his khaki shooting jacket.

It was after all this revelry, when the pale sun was well down the sky, that the tragedy of the day occurred.

The Band had been exploring on their skates new bogs of the seemingly endless chain that stretched away through the woods. The last one was shut in by trees, and seemed deeper and with more springs beneath its surface, which made the smooth ice bend and crack ominously at times. Yet it was the most beautiful of all. Where grass stems had touched the ice, dainty flowers of hoarfrost made wonderful patterns as if etched in rippled glass. Here and there were sheets of ice of a deep gleaming blue like that dread "paved work of a sapphire stone" about which the Band had read last Sunday.

It was Honey, the adventurer, who discovered a new speedway, a long ditch at the far end of the bog, shadowed by sweet gum trees, stretching between banks of aronia or chokeberries, both red and black, which were carpeted with the wine-red pyxie and the trailing cranberry vine with their leaves of crimson-lake, and here and there a scarlet berry overlooked by the pickers. Down the glimmering stretch he sped in spite of the Captain's warning shout. Suddenly just ahead gleamed a stretch of clear water where a spring bubbled up. The ice was so transparent that Honey never glimpsed the difference until close to the edge. He tried desperately to stop; but one of his skates chose that moment of all others to come off, and poor Honey fell flat on the cracking ice which, just as the Captain reached him, broke with a snap.

Honey went up to his shoulders in the icy water, but grasping the Captain's long hockey stick was pulled out on the ice in a second. Immediately the water began to freeze, until Honey's clothes clanked as he walked. The Captain pulled off his skates, poured the water out of his dripping shoes, and gave the long wailing owl call, the Band's signal of distress. They hurried up from different parts of the bog to find Honey trying hard to smile a wan watery smile, a difficult performance over chattering teeth.

The Captain laced up the wet shoes again, wrapped his dry sweater around Honey's shivering shoulders, and, holding his wet hand in his, loped off for the cabin two long miles away, leaving the Third to convoy Henny-Penny and Alice-Palace, while Trottie raced back and forth between the van and the rear.

"P-o-o-r Honey," pitied Alice-Palace, "was he trying to catch a turtie?"

"He hasn't cried a bit," reported Trottie to Henny-Penny, whose sensitive nature frequently took refuge in tears. Henny-Penny was much impressed.

"Not even a littly bit?" he inquired anxiously. "Didn't he make a whimpy noise?"

"I didn't cry neither," boasted Alice-Palace, "when I falled down. I was going to," she confessed, "but then I sawed some nice dear turties under the ice and I forgot to."

It was a long, cold two miles for Honey, even though cheered by condolences and conversation from the rear-guard; but the Cabin was sighted at last. It did not take the Captain a minute to start a roaring fire in the ten-foot fireplace. Honey's wet things were peeled off in a jiffy, and he was rubbed down with a big scratchy towel until he turned pink all over. Then, swathed in a fuzzy warm bathrobe, he sleepily watched his steaming clothes dry while the Captain brewed another pot of cocoa.

Two hours later the Band were home, and horrifying Mother with tales of tumbles, turtles, campfires, rescues, and other harrowing adventures by field and flood.

"You're all so little," she complained, hugging as many of them as she could reach, "it's too dangerous."

"No-o-o, Muvvy, we love it!" said Henny-Penny and Alice-Palace together.

"Not with the Captain along," asserted Trottie, holding tight to one of his hands, while Honey and the Third divided the other.

Mother gave the Captain a long look—quite a nice look it was.

"Well, perhaps not," she admitted at last.

THE FOX FAMILY

It all began with a loose tooth. Said tooth was the property of Alice-Palace, and when it became very wobbly indeed she allowed Mother to take it out and never even made a cry face. Thereafter the tooth was placed under her pillow and by the next morning had changed into a bright, shiny dime as is the way with the lost loose teeth of good, brave children. Then came the important and vital question as to what should be the investment of this fund. It was Henny-Penny, her twin, who first aroused Alice-Palace to the necessity of prompt action.

"S'pose," he began ominously, "that a big old, bad old burglar should come some night an' climb up to our window?"

"S'pose he should," agreed Alice-Palace, her eyes getting bigger and bigger.

"An s'pose he should open the window and come creepy, creepy along the floor right to your crib?"

"S'pose he did," agreed Alice-Palace very faintly.

"An' s'pose," continued the inspired Henny, "that he'd grab you in the dark and yell, 'Gimme that dime!'"

This climax was too much for Alice-Palace and she raised her voice several feet on high and rushed down the stairs to Mother, followed by the overwrought Henny-Penny who had firmly convinced himself that the abovementioned burglar was actually in one of the dark corners of the nursery. It was some time before the tumult and the shouting died down sufficiently for Mother to find out what it was all about. The very next day Alice-Palace decided not to take any further chances in keeping so large a sum of money in the house. Henny-Penny generously offered to allow her to deposit it in his dime savings bank, which was guaranteed to open on the dropping in of fifty dimes. As he was still forty-seven short of the opening coin the prospect did not appeal to his twin. Honey suggested ten sticks of candy, to be nobly divided among the different members of the Band. Trottie rather leaned toward an ice cream cone, which could be distributed by alternate licks among her comrades at arms. The important question was finally put up to the Captain.

"Buy a tree," he advised without an instant's hesitation. "Next to bringing up a nice girl or a boy," he explained, "there is nothing that is better than to plant a tree and watch it growing bigger and better every year. There are lots of places," he confided, "where I have planted trees and I never go by any of them without stopping to look at my tree and see how it is getting along. Only the other day," he went on, "I was near a little house in the city, with a brick-paved backyard about as big as a pocket handkerchief. Mother and I lived there once before the Band began. One day I took up four bricks and planted a tulip tree. Yesterday I stopped there and my tree had grown higher than the house and made that little, stuffy, hot backyard all cool and green."

Accordingly, that very afternoon the whole Band started for a nursery some three miles away, over by Darby Creek, where a dime would buy a good pin oak seedling. The beginning of twilight found them marching in single file through Fox Valley, Alice-Palace holding her precious tree clasped tightly in both hands. They had stopped at a tiny dark pool on the edge of Blacksnake Swamp, where the Captain showed them a vast pin oak tree seventy-five feet tall and so large around that the whole Band, except the Captain, could hardly encircle it with their joined hands. The Captain told Alice-Palace that was about the way her pin oak would look to her great, great grandchildren.

It was a gray, cold afternoon as they followed a winding trail through the beech woods that crossed the brook and then wound its way along a little wooded valley. The Band were marching without a sound, for the Captain had taught them that it is bad manners to make any noise in the woods. The wild-folk, he said, did not like noise, and the woods belong to them. Suddenly the Captain, who was walking a little ahead, turned and held up his hand and pointed with the other like a semaphore. Down the opposite slope through the trees some fifty feet away trotted wearily a gaunt old mother fox. As the Third said afterwards, she looked exactly like the pictures of the wolf in Red Riding Hood.

Close behind her padded a round woolly little cub with such a funny little face that it was all the children could do to keep from laughing every time they looked at him. He was reddish, but with two long stripes of gray down his breast and across his round little tummy. Another larger cub came from among the trees to meet them. He evidently had a bad temper, for he snarled at his little brother and then suddenly turned and disappeared down a deep burrow which the Band noticed for the first time had been dug under the roots of a great oak tree. On looking closely they could see two other burrows in a line with the first, one under a rock and the other in the slope of a bank. Between the three ran a well-trodden path and behind them all lay an enormous dead chestnut log. The old mother fox trotted over to the log, lay down on the very top with her magnificent brush hanging down to one side, dropped her keen, sharp, sly face into her paws—and fell asleep. The little woolly cub trotted sedately over to the middle burrow and lay down on a tiny bank of earth. Like human cubs he evidently did not care much about taking a nap. First he ate a few blades of grass. Then catching sight of a dry leaf which stuck upright in his woolly fur, he twisted himself around and around, trying to catch it with his teeth, and finally rolled over and over, with the result that when he stopped he had three leaves in his fur instead of one.

In front of him was the corpse of a battered old black crow. He would steal up toward this with the utmost caution, without a sound, and finally spring through the air and land right on top of the unsuspecting crow, which he would proceed to worry and shake with fierce little growls and yaps, something like those made by a puppy, only much sharper. At last he too lay down and curling himself into a round ball with his funny little head on his paws went fast asleep. The wind was blowing from the foxes toward the Band or this never would have happened.

For a long time they all stood stony still, looking first at the mother fox and then at the cub. Finally the Captain tiptoed his way up the slope. Although he made hardly a sound that the Band could hear, yet he had not gone three steps before the little cub sprang up with wide open eyes and looked straight at him. The Captain stood perfectly still, with one foot out in the very act of making a step. A wild animal cannot tell by sight a man from a tree if only he stands still, and in a minute the cub lay down and went to sleep. Once more the Captain started, and the same thing happened again and again, until at last he was scarcely twenty feet away from the cub. Suddenly the mother fox was standing right beside the cub. Not one of the Band had seen her come. Her keen, fierce, sly face peered through the trees trying to find what had made the tiny sound which had brought her down from the watchtower. Nothing but the eyes of the Band moved, yet when they looked back from the cub the old mother-fox was gone as silently as she had come.

Once more the little cub lay down and seemed to fall fast asleep. This time, however, he must have been watching through half shut eyes, for at the very first movement that the Captain made he started up again and in a very slow and dignified manner, as if he had suddenly remembered something, he turned and disappeared in the middle burrow. The Band hurried up and joined the Captain. They found that the big log above the burrows was worn smooth, showing that Mrs. Fox must have used it often. In front of the burrows were the feathers of flickers, grackles, bits of rabbit fur, and the battered old crow aforesaid. The Captain told them that every fox warren had a secret entrance which was only used to go in or out in great emergencies. For a long time the Band looked and looked, but could find nothing except the three holes in plain sight. Finally Trottie saw a single reddish hair clinging to the edge of a hollow stump. Looking inside he discovered that a hole had been dug down through the decayed wood and into the ground beyond, making the secret entrance.

The Captain told them that probably Mrs. Fox would move with all her children that very night, for foxes are jealous of letting humans know where they live. That was just what happened, for never again did the Band meet any of the fox-family there. Indeed, the last time they visited the place a big fat stupid woodchuck was living in one of the burrows.

THE LOST LAND

They have sought him high, they have sought him low,
They have sought him over down and lea;
They have found him by the milk-white thorn
That guards the gates o' Faerie.

'Twas bent beneath and blue above,
Their eyes were held that they might not see
The kine that grazed beneath the knowes,
Oh, they were the Queens o' Faerie.

So read the Captain from the "Rhyme of True Thomas" to the Band in the flickering firelight.
"I wish we could find Fairyland!" sighed Honey after a while.

"The way was lost thousands and thousands of years ago and we are all so busy and hurried and worried nowadays that most of us never find it," Captain said.

"Couldn't little girls who aren't hurried or worried go there?" inquired Alice-Palace from her corner.

"And nice, good, quite big boys, too," added her twin, Henny-Penny, anxiously, from his.

"Pooh!" said the sophisticated Trottie, "there isn't any such place."

"Well," meditated the Third, who usually understood the Captain better than the rest of the Band, "I know what Fathy means. It's where little people like birds and orchids and funny old animals live."

"Well," said the Captain, "it's bedtime now, but if you'll be down tomorrow morning fifteen minutes after you hear the Call, we'll see what we can find."

At the first robin song, which always comes just when the stars begin to grow dim in the east, there sounded the clear whistle of the cardinal grosbeak from the Captain's room. As the sun came up, the whole Band were on the march. By midmorning, they were in a new country. The woods looked like a shimmering pool of changing greens, lapping over a white sand land that had been thrust up from the south into the very heart of the north. They followed a wood path to a little cabin nestled among the pitch pines on the high bank of a stream stained brown and steeped sweet with a million cedar roots. By the rail, a mountain laurel raised a ghost-like glory of white, pink flecked flowers. Over the low door hung a tiny bog iron horseshoe dug up in a cranberry bog and undoubtedly cast by some fairy steed.

After a wonderful lunch on the wide, cool porch which overhung the stream, the Band pushed on through a tangle of tiny trees—the leaves of which had a sharp, small thorn at each angle, and which the Captain told the Band were scrub oaks: the smallest of their family. The Captain pushed aside branches of withewood, with its flat masses of white bloom and star-leaved sweet gum saplings, until finally, through the underbrush, appeared a faint path. The woods became very still and no one felt like speaking. The path crept in and out through the marshes until it came to the very edge of the bank of the creek. Suddenly, at the Captain's feet, the Band saw something which made them stand and look for a long time without a word. Out of the center of a mass of hollow, crimson-streaked leaves filled with clear water, swung two glorious blossoms. Wine-red, aquamarine, pearl-white and pale gold gleamed the twin flowers that nodded proudly to the children from the ends of long, slender stems.

"It's the pitcher plant," whispered the Captain as the Band bent down to look more closely at these marsh dwellers.

From the stream, the hidden path wound through thicket after thicket, sweet as spring, with the fragrance of the wild magnolia and the spicery of the gray-green bayberry. Its bed was made of white sea sand. By its side spread the vivid crimson-lake leaves of the wild ipecac, with its strange green flowers, and everywhere, as if set in snow, gleamed the green and gold of the Barrens heather. The plants looked like tiny cedar trees loaded down with thickly set blossoms of pure gold which the wind spilled in little yellow drifts on the sand. In the distance through the trees came glimpses of far away meadows, hazy purple with blue toadflax. Beside the path showed here and there the pale gold of the narrow-leafed sundrops with a center of deep orange stamens. Beyond were masses of lambskill, with its fatal leaves and crimson blossoms. On and on, the path led. Past jade green pools, in which gleamed buds of the yellow pond lily, like lumps of floating gold. Among these were the paler golden club, which looked like the tongue of the calla lily. At last, the path stretched straight toward a flat-topped mound that showed dim and fair through the low trees. The Captain halted the Band.

"That may be one of the fairy hills," he whispered.

"Like the one where the man heard them sing inside?" queried Henny-Penny.

"Yes," answered the Captain, "just such a one. 'Robin Adair,' you know, that Mother sometimes sings to you," he went on, "is a fairy song that a shepherd heard and learned at twilight coming from inside a fairy hill."

The Band closed up close and crept along in perfect silence. Just before the mound, in a tangle of sand myrtle with vivid little oval green leaves and feathery white, pink-centered blossoms, stood a bush with a pale gray trunk and leaves of bright arsenic green.

"Be careful," warned the Captain, pushing aside the vivid foliage, "don't let those leaves touch you. They are the fingers of a bad fairy and her name is Poison Sumac."

"Aren't you afraid of her?" asked Trottie, as the Band filed around the bush.

"No," said the Captain, "I must have had a fairy godmother, for Poison Ivy and Poison Sumac don't hurt me."

As the Captain let the fierce branches fall back into place, Henny-Penny pushed on ahead along the path. Just as he came to a sharp bend where the way turned toward the mound, a fierce, deep hiss sounded from beyond. Poor Henny-Penny scuttled back, his face fairly white with terror.

"There's an norful big old, bad old snake right across the path," he panted.

"That's only another sentry," the Captain reassured him. "He only hurts those who are afraid of him."

The Captain strode along the path and bent down and raised the great body of a pine snake, cream-white and umber-brown and fully six feet long. At first, the snake raised its strange, pointed head with its gold and black eyes and hissed fearfully, but when it found that the Captain meant no harm, it coiled contentedly around his arm and accompanied the Band into the enchanted circle, where the pyxies had carpeted the sand with their wine-red and green moss, starred thick with hundreds of flat five-petaled white blossoms.

"Men have traveled hundreds of miles," the Captain told them, "to see a piece of this pyxie moss, which isn't moss at all, but just a little shrub."

Near the summit of the mound, the path was lost in a foam of the blue, lilac and white butterfly blossoms of the lupine. Little clouds of fragrance drifted through the air as the wind swung rows and rows of the transparent

bells of the leucothoe. Beyond the lupine stood a rank
of dazzling white turkey beards. The inmost circle of
the mound was carpeted with dry gray reindeer moss,
into which the feet of the Band sank deep. Right before
them, like crinkled globes of jacinth, drooped on slender
stems, were seven rose-red moccasin flowers, one of the
most beautiful of all the orchids. In the still sunlight,
the Band looked at them long.

"I guess," whispered Alice-Palace at last, "they must
be the Seven Queens of Fairyland. If we had only come
quicker and quieter, we would have seen them."

THE BIRDLERS

"Fathy's a great birdler," complimented Alice-Palace, as the Captain explained to the Band the difference between the black-and-white warbler and the white-breasted nuthatch. Both of them run up and down trees, but the "topnotch," as Alice-Palace insisted on calling the nuthatch, had white cheeks and a grunting note, while the warbler was streaked black and white and sang a little creaking song. The Band were at the Cabin in the piniest part of the Pine Barrens, whose snowy sand and white pebbles harked back to the days when they were the bed of some sea, forgotten a hundred thousand years ago. They had come over to find certain birds which were not seen on their side of the Delaware River. The Band took their bird study very seriously. Each one of them kept a life list and a year list beside their day lists, in which they set down the name and date of each bird met. The one who could tell forty different kinds of birds in a single day won a pair of field glasses. Then, too, they all kept notes. Even Alice-Palace, who was only six, carried an enormous blank book about the size of a geography. To date, it contained this single note: "Robbins eat Wormes. I saw him do it. I wouldn't."

They had just finished the largest breakfast ever eaten by a military organization. At least, so said Mother, who had charge of the Commissary as well as the Ambulance Corps. From over the creek came a sort of squealing cry that sounded like escaping steam. A hawk, with a barred tail and white underneath except for the black tips of its underwings, swept by overhead. It was the broad-winged hawk, which eats snakes and mice and is one of the good hawks. In fact, the Captain told the Band that they are all good, from the red-tailed down to the small sparrow hawk, except one—the fatal little sharp-shinned hawk. He it was, who last winter followed the Captain's gallant company of evening grosbeaks down from the frozen North cutting out one a day until by April there were only scattered remnants of the largest flock ever reported. It is he who is the destruction that wasteth at noonday for so many happy little useful birds. The Captain's bird lecture at this point was cut short by a squeal of distress from Alice-Palace. She had slipped away during the talk to a nearby thicket from which she returned on the run, with angry looking stings on the back of both hands. In the middle distance a little cloud of yellow striped insects buzzed sullenly around a hole by a little tussock.

"I was taming yellow jackets and they bited me," sobbed Alice-Palace.

While the Band was comforting Alice with sympathy and wet clay, Henny-Penny, her twin, decided to take prompt action against the ungrateful insects. Armed with a water bucket, he waited near the nest until the last yellow jacket had buzzed his way in. Then, suddenly clapping the pail upside down over the hole, he sat on it while the yellow jackets fizzed inside like a soda fountain. He had overlooked the fact, however, that some of the swarm were away from home. In a moment, he was sharply reminded of their return and tore back to the Cabin, joining his laments to those of his twin until, as Trottie said, the camp sounded like a massacre.

"Comrades," said the harassed Captain when order had been restored, "let us be on our way. Anywhere but here. Nothing can be worse than this. Forward march!"

In single file, amid the snifflings of the wounded, the Band moved away, following a path which led through brilliant masses of the Carolina pink and by clumps of the birdfoot violet, like patches of blue sky which had drifted down to earth. On either side were thickets of sand myrtle and shadblow, blueberry and cassandra all in blossom. For some distance, the path ran beside the rushing waters of Stop the Jade Stream. The Captain had them notice a curious thing. All of the brooks in the Pine Barrens were silent. None of them sang and chattered as in the North. This was because there were no stones in their beds and they ran through deep soft sand.

Suddenly a little bird with two white wing bars and a blue-gray head spoke from out of a pine tree. "See-see! me-ee! you-you!" he sang. It was the solitary or blue-headed vireo on his way to the mountains, rarest of his family except the almost unknown Philadelphia vireo. Later in the day the Band heard the white-eyed vireo. "Whip Tom Kelly! Whip Tom Kelly!" he cried explosively from the brook bank. The path wound its way deeper and deeper into the dry, sweet woods. Here and there were little clumps of wild ipecac. Henny-Penny regarded the herb shudderingly. Once when he was young—it must have been all of two years before—he had found Honey's paint box one morning unguarded before breakfast. It was a hungry time of day and the paints looked tasty. A few minutes later, there was only a nibbled bit of crimson-lake left in the whole box. Thereafter, Doctor Bellows and a dose of ipecac played a prompt part in the adventure—all of which accounted for Henny-Penny's failure to appreciate ipecac, either growing or bottled.

It was at the Upper Dam that the Band met the two birds they had especially hoped to find. It was Honey who saw the first. Flitting through the scrub oaks and gleaming in and out among the young leaves was one of the most brilliant of all the warblers. Its breast was sunshine-yellow, with black streaks down the sides, and it had a yellow spot under the eye, yellowish wing bars, and a greenish back; it sang a song made up of thin, wiry notes that ran up the scale. This was the prairie warbler, a bird that loves scrub oaks and dry thickets and builds a little jewel casket of a nest all lined with soft brown fern wool. A few minutes later, Trottie heard what sounded like a chipping sparrow trilling away in the woods and caught sight of the other Pine Barren bird, the pine warbler.

It was a larger bird than the prairie, with a greenish back, a bright yellow throat and breast, and white wing bars. The Captain told the Band that for years and years he had searched for the pine warbler's nest, but had never yet found it. Once in the late afternoon, he had met Mrs. Pine Warbler with some sticks in her mouth, but there was only time to catch his train and he had to go without watching her. She never gave him another chance.

The best bird adventure of all came last. The Band was coming back to the Cabin tired and hot, but with a list of over forty birds when they came to a little clearing near Lower Mill. On the ground hopped a bird with a reddish-brown back and head, a white breast heavily spotted with black. It was the wood thrush, a rare bird in the Barrens. Near him was a smaller, lighter thrush of a tawny brown color, with its breast and throat lightly spotted with tawny brown spots.

"It's the veery," said the Captain, "side by side with the wood thrush."

"There's another," whispered Trottie, "on the ground just beyond."

As he spoke, a still smaller thrush, with its head, back and wings of an olive-brown, hopped from the ground to a low twig and the whole Band could see that its tail was of a reddish-brown quite different from the color of its back.

"Watch its tail," said the Captain.

Sure enough in a minute the bird slowly raised its tail until it stuck out at an angle to its back like the tail of a wren.

"It's a hermit thrush," said the Captain, "though he is passing through late. You can always tell him by the reddish tail and his funny trick of raising it when he is embarrassed."

In a nearby tree, a robin sang and the Captain said that he was a thrush, too, and was sometimes called the migratory thrush. Then from overhead came the sky call of the bluebird, the smallest of all of our thrushes. So the Band had been lucky enough to see at the same time five of the eight thrushes, only the olive-backed, the gray-cheeked, and the Bicknell's thrush being absent.

The adventure was not over yet. Just as the Band was moving off, the hermit thrush hopped to a higher branch and began to sing. Not once in years does one hear the hermit thrush sing in migration, and the whole Band stood still as stones. The song was the whisper song which the hermit thrush sings to himself before trying the full throated song of the nesting season. Up and up went the pure-fluted notes, the higher ones with just a little tremolo at the end. There were no bass notes, as in the song of the wood thrush. Finally, when the highest notes sounded, the song seemed to stop, but there in front of them was the bird still singing, its beak opening and shutting, and its whole body quivering in an ecstasy. The song had passed beyond the range of human ears. Only the singer and the wild folk for whom he sang could hear the best part of the hermit thrush's song.

"Won't we ever hear it?" said Alice-Palace.

"Someday," said the Captain, "we'll hear all the music that we can't hear now.

THE OWL CALL

The bird migration month of May was past and the Band were now spending most of their spare time birds-nesting. Every afternoon after school and all day on Saturdays, they would hunt and hunt. Whenever they found a nest, each of them wrote in their blank bird book when and where it was found, what it was made of, how many eggs there were, how they looked, how the parent birds looked, what they did, what they said—there were lots and lots of things to set down. Then the Third, who had a new camera, would take a photograph of the nest and each of the Band would paste a print of it in their bird book. Then, they would visit the different nests as often as they could and write down what they saw. The Captain said that notes on nests and birds were always valuable. Anybody might find out something, even from the most ordinary nest, that had never been known before. That was the reason, he said, why all the great ornithologists of the country were so anxious to have people make notes about the birds. Only, he told the Band, they must write down only what they were sure they saw and heard and never guess at anything. He said, too, that this was a much better way of collecting than taking the nests and eggs, for that was like spending principal. There would never be any more income from the nests, such as the fun of visiting them and showing them to other bird lovers, and seeing the young birds when they came, and watching them be fed. Then, too, each egg taken meant one bird less, and nearly every bird was worth a dollar a year to the farmers because of the insects and weed seeds it ate.

The Captain had promised to show them how to find a meadowlark's nest, for which they had hunted many times in the pasture without success. Taking a long string, he tied one end to Trottie's left and the other to Honey's right leg, just above the ankle. They moved out until the cord was taut, and then started across the meadow. The string touched the top of the long grass over a space of nearly a hundred feet. The rest of the Band and the Captain deployed out and followed behind. They had not gone twenty yards when right in front of the swishing cord, a brown streaked bird flew up. The Band dashed to the place and there, fastened to the long grasses and touching the ground, was a nest made of weed stalks lined with grass and holding five pale blue eggs, all scrawled and spotted with strange dark purple and black marks. The streaked bird and a magnificent black bird, which wore a scarlet epaulette on each shoulder, edged with buff and white, flew around and around, making sharp, scolding notes. It was the nest of the red-winged blackbird, which more often builds on a tussock or in a low bush in swamps than on the ground. The Band took a recess to write up their bird books and then started the drag again. On the slope of a little hill, a big brown bird with a bright yellow breast with a black crescent on it sprang from the grass and glided away showing white tail feathers as it flew. Again, the Band rushed to the spot where the bird had flown up, but hunt as they would, they could find no nest.

"Look back of the string," said the Captain. "This bird usually runs away from its nest before it flies."

The Band took his advice, and fully ten feet from where the sly bird started up, Henny-Penny found on the ground a big nest made of woven grass arched over in front, holding five large white eggs speckled thick with reddish-brown spots. When the Band had finished writing up this find, it was getting towards supper time and the Captain decided to bivouac in the New Forest. The Forest was a wood of beech trees between two round green hills that the Captain had once discovered. At its very heart was a bubbling spring of clear water that never froze in winter, nor failed in summer. At the edge of the wood was the Haunted House, which the Band planned to explore someday when they all felt unusually brave.

As soon as they entered the Forest, the whole Band changed. Henny-Penny became Will Scarlet,

Alice-Palace was Maid Marion. The Captain wanted to be Robin Hood, but the Band unkindly decided that he was built on the exact lines of Friar Tuck. Trottie was appointed Robin Hood over all other competitors because of the fact that he alone could wind a hunting horn. It was carried in his pocket and looked much like a whistle. The Third, as the tallest, became Little John and Honey was Allan a'Dale. Thus changed, the Band followed a dim path fringed with white thorn bloom and sprays of sweet viburnum. Against the amber afterglow showed the faint tracery of the late leafing beeches. As the path wound its way among the white bare boles, the woods had the effect of a sudden silence.

"They've stopped talking," said Robin Hood in a hushed voice.

"Who?" queried Will Scarlet in a startled whisper.

"Oh—They," Robin said, mysteriously, and the Band, with one accord, closed up around the Friar, while a little hand that seemed to belong to that dashing blade, Will Scarlet, slipped into one of his. At last, the gallant company reached a bank all blue and white with enameled innocents. In front was the bare path on which the camp fire was always kindled. The Band scattered for firewood, although not far, for there were too many lurking shadows among those tree trunks. Then came the Lighting of the Camp Fire. This was always the duty of Friar Tuck. Time was when he had done his devoir with a flint arrowhead, an old file and tinder made from a half charred rag and carried in the shell of a Mauser cartridge. Having thus given the Band a taste of his real quality as a woodsman, he had, however, gone back to the more prosaic safety match. It was the Rule of the Camp Fire that the Fire lighter must be limited to one match. If so be that he failed, the honor descended to Little John and so on in succession down to Maid Marion, the newest recruit. The Friar took no chances. With great care, he selected four dry beech leaves and broke a handful of tiny dry twigs from a nearby hornbeam. The leaves were crumpled into a ball and over this, a little tepee was built from twigs. Above this were crisscrossed layers of beech and black oak branches and then, with this structure as a hub, was built a wheel of heavy beech, hornbeam, red cedar and white oak limbs—all of which make a hot, clear flame and good coals for cooking.

When the fire was built at last to the Friar's liking, he knelt down on the windward side, match in hand. It was a tense moment. The match sputtered and Little John and Robin Hood anxiously watched a tongue of flame creep up through the leaf ball to the dry twigs. It would be unworthy of their fair fame to say that they hoped that, for once, the tiny flame would flicker and die out in darkness. Probably the sigh that they heaved when the inner pyre of twigs at last turned into a heart of fire was one of relief rather than of disappointment. At any rate, five minutes later, all powers of darkness fled for their lives before the steady roaring column of smokeless flame that surged up.

Followed feasting and wassail. Great haunches of venison broiled hissingly at the end of green hornbeam spits and tasted much like muttonchops. Flagons of Adam's ale were quaffed, and there was song and story while the loving cup—it was of the folding variety—passed from hand to hand. Then as the fire died down to the steady glow of red embers, the Band moved in closer while the Friar related, without undue modesty, divers of his adventures by field and flood. Thereafter, Allan a'Dale recited sundry selections from the "Lay of the Last Minstrel," recently memorized after school as a penalty for things ill done and undone. It must have been the tale of that wondrous wizard, Michael Scott and his book of gramarie, that started the Friar on a quest for renown.

"Hist," he said impressively, and heaved himself up beside the dying fire.

There was not a sound in the sleeping forest. Wood folk, water folk—all were still. Then, from the pursed lips of the Friar came a long, wavering, mournful call. Sad it was, with a certain eerie wildness of quality, like a lonely wind shrilling at midnight through gaunt branches. Again and again, the sound shuddered away across the neighboring hills. Suddenly, so far away that at first it seemed an echo, it was answered. Again and again, the call sounded and each time the answer came nearer and louder, and it was evident that whatever had been called was coming fast.

Then suddenly across the firelight drifted a dark form with fiery eyes and silent wings. With one accord the Band threw themselves on the Friar, who rocked under the impact.

"Oo-oo-oo!" observed Maid Marion loudly.

"Don't do it any more, Fathy," wailed Will Scarlet.

"Can't you stop It comin'?" inquired Allan a' Dale, anxiously.

"Oughtn't we to draw a circle around the fire?" whispered Robin Hood.

"No, a pen-pen-pentacle," stuttered Little John.

The Friar stopped.

"I am surprised, Comrades," he said severely. "You aren't afraid of an old screech owl, are you?"

"N-n-n-o," quavered Will Scarlet, "if you're sure it's a nowl."

"Certain sure," asserted the Friar, and gave the call again, this time with a long tremolo note at the end.

Around and around the light, but never across it, skimmed the owl, and ever it gave its cry, the sweetest, weirdest of all the night notes. Finally, it lighted on a near-by tree and began a little crooning call—the love song of its kind, which the Friar could only approximate. It waited for an answer, giving at times another little squawking note, which was also beyond the Friar. At last, disgusted with his clumsy attempts to continue a conversation so well begun, it melted silently away into the darkness.

Anything after that performance would be an anti-climax, the Band felt. Water was poured on the blaze and earth heaped over the hissing embers, and under the sullen flare of Antares and Arcturus, the Band started homeward through dim wood roads and flower-scented lanes. Will Scarlet and Maid Marion frankly claimed either hand of the Friar, and in the darkest places, even the redoubtable Robin himself casually took possession of an unoccupied thumb.

THE BEST NEST

"Comrades," said the Captain one Monday morning at breakfast, "I have an announcement to make. Next Saturday afternoon a noble hearted philanthropist has offered to give a prize to the one of the Band who can show at that time the most interesting nest. The judge of the contest will be the Quartermaster-General, sometimes known as Mother."

Henny-Penny piped up, "Who's the philoranthroperist?"

"For certain military reasons," said the Captain darkly, "he wishes his name to remain unknown."

"What's the prize?" the practical Honey-Bee demanded.

"It'll be something well worth winning," the Captain responded mysteriously, "if only you do your part."

"I know where there's a nice, wriggly, worm's nest," announced Alice-Palace, "full of squirmy baby worms in a napple tree."

"No," said Mother firmly, "wriggly worms' nests are barred."

Every spare hour of the next six days was given over to huntings and scurryings and secrets. By Saturday, each member of the Band was acting very puffly and important, and it was plain that every single one of them expected to win the prize. The Interesting Nest Competition was scheduled to begin at two thirty, on the arrival of the Captain's train. As the great Salamanca Bell of the clock tower of Wentworth Farm, which sets the time for miles around, chimed the half hour, the whole band was drawn up at the foot of Violet Hill to meet the Captain. Besides the Quartermaster-General, there were the Reserves, consisting of Aunt Alice and Uncle Jack, and Minnie and Annie of the Commissary Department, and John the gardener, of the Engineers' Corps, relieved from trench duty that afternoon, beside a number of miscellaneous civilians who were allowed occasionally to attend a review of the Band. Suddenly down the road sounded the call of the cardinal grosbeak. A minute later, the Captain himself appeared around a corner of the shrubbery.

The Third led off. Down Violet Hill, across the lawn, along the curving driveway and through the great stone gates he went, followed by the Band and their camp followers. Up Roberts Road, he led them to where the sidewalk ran directly under a squatty dogwood tree which, naturally, the Band had learned to tell by its bark. Not five feet from the ground was a crotch where four large branches shot out from the main trunk. Probably fifty people had passed directly under this tree that day, including the Captain, and most of the procession, for it was on the road which led to the station. No one but the Third had ever noticed that over the edge of the crotch, a couple of straws showed together with what looked like a sharp-pointed, yellowish thorn. Reaching up his finger, the Third touched the thorn. Immediately, with an indignant chirp, a mother robin flew out. The thorn had been her beak, just showing over the edge of the mud nest which she had built slyly to fit a deep hollow in the crotch. So silently had she brooded over the four turquoise-blue eggs, which gleamed out of the grass-lined nest that no one save the Third had even suspected what was there. One by one, the Band and the visitors filed past and took turns at peeping into the nest. The Judge came last.

"It's a dear nest," she said, smiling into the Third's eyes, which were as blue as the eggs.

With a couple of reproachful chirps, Mrs. Robin took her place again in the nest and the march was resumed.

"Nothing but an old robin's nest," scoffed Trottie, who came next. "Come along with me and I'll show you a real nest."

Back again up the hill, past the white oak tree and clear down into the pasture where the windmill stood, they went. Part of the pasture, which sloped down to the brook, had been plowed up for corn and the plowed land came nearly to a rail fence, along which Trottie led the Band. He stopped in front of a little stake which he had stuck into the hard ground just beyond the last furrow.

"Gee!" he shouted excitedly a second later.

"They've hatched!"

The Band and the visitors crowded up to see. From a little hollow in the crumbling side of the narrow belt of turf along the fence was pouring a procession of tiny turtles, each one about the size of a twenty-five cent piece. Unerringly and unhesitatingly, they marched out from the nest and across the long, plowed field in the straightest possible line to the brook. Behind the vanguard, some were even then just struggling out of long, white, cylindrical eggs with tough parchment-like shells. The unhurrying, unhesitating little turtles paid no attention to the squeals of the Band or to the crowd of faces which bent down toward them. Trottie told the interested Judge how he had found old, fierce Mrs. Snapping Turtle just coming out of the nest, which she had made by forcing the back end of her shell into the side of the tiny bank. As she came out, the earth fell in after her and covered up to exactly the right depth the handful of snowy eggs which she had laid.

"That's a very interesting nest, too," said the Judge, pulling one of Trottie's floppy ears as he pointed out to her every last detail of his discovery.

From the pasture, Honey-Bee hurried them to the Linden Walk. There, two avenues of linden trees came together at a right angle and made a shaded spot on the hottest summer day. Down the cool path, Honey-Bee led them. The branches of the lindens, with their funny lopsided leaves, bent down until they almost touched the ground. About the middle of one of the walks, Honey stopped and pushed through the crooked branches until he reached the open lawn beyond. From a little fork of an outer branch overhung by leaves swung a tiny woven basket. It was made of fine, tough grass and thatched on the outside with white strips of birch bark and bits of spider silk. Inside, the nest was lined with the fine needles of the white pine. Over the edge of the nest peeped the head of a little bird with a tiny hooked beak—the field mark of the vireo. Above its eye was a white stripe with a black stripe just below, while the iris of the eye itself was of a dark red color—all of which marked the bird as the red-eyed vireo. As the party came nearer and nearer, the little bird shifted uneasily, and several times started to fly.

Finally, however, it gave one look around as if to say, "I'm going to guard these eggs whatever happens," and snuggled down close into the nest, refusing even to move. Honey-Bee put his hand out very slowly and stroked the trembling little gray back. At that, Mrs. Vireo pecked his finger like a little setting hen, and then cuddled her head trustfully up against it. Honey-Bee finally persuaded her to perch on the rim of the nest so that the Judge could see the four eggs like pink pearls, spotted with reddish-brown at the larger end. The moment her visitors moved away, she went back to her eggs with a contented little chirp.

"What do you think of that for a nest?" exulted Honey to Mother as Henny-Penny took the lead.

"One of the most interesting that I've seen," said the latter judicially, and that was all that Honey-Bee could get out of her.

Henny-Penny led the Band, civilians, camp followers and all, straight to the house. Across the wide
veranda and through the broad doorway, they marched
and up the curving staircase which stopped to rest every
few steps at comfortable, deep-set landings.

"It must be a mouse's nest," suggested Trottie as
they filed down the hall toward Henny-Penny's room.

"Or a spider's," said the Third. Not a word could
they get out of Henny-Penny.

Across his room he took them, past yards of electric
railway tracks and wonderfully constructed machines,
made out of blocks, spools, nails, and odds and ends of
pipe. Not until he reached the open window did he stop.

"There," he said, waving a pudgy hand triumphantly
toward what seemed to be a knot on a limb of a spread-
ing sugar maple tree which came close to the house.

It was only when they all looked at it closely that
they saw that it was not a knot, but really a tiny nest
saddled on a small twig and covered with lichens. The
opening of the nest was just about the size of a twenty-five cent piece. The nest itself was lined with the
softest of brown and white wool, which the Captain said
came from ferns. On the outside, it was thickly thatched
with tiny pieces of green lichens and bound around and
around in a network of cobwebs, which not only lashed
it to the limb, but stitched it solidly together. Inside were
two tiny, long white eggs. Even as everybody crowded
up to the window seat to see, there came a hum and a
vivid green tiny bird with a long-curved beak swooped
down upon the nest in front of their very eyes. It was

the mother ruby-throated hummingbird, which lacks the ruby throat. For a long time, everybody watched and admired the nest and the tiny beautiful bird.

"Mothy," piped Henny-Penny as they started down the stairs again, "that's the bestest of 'em all. Isn't it?" But the Judge only smiled and rumpled Henny-Penny's tousled brown hair.

"Humph!" said Alice-Palace, making a pout face.

"You come see my nest. It isn't any crawly turtle's or old bird's nest, but it's better'n all of them."

Down the stairs and through the door, they all marched again. Straight across the lawn, Alice-Palace led them. Just ahead of them, through the shrubbery suddenly darted a brown rabbit, showing her white powderpuff with every jump. On the grass not five feet away from a side of the house, Alice stopped. Just ahead of her lay two dry leaves. Stooping down, she started to pick these up when, again, the same brown bunny came circling around her, so close that it could almost be touched. Underneath the leaves was a tuft of brown wool. Lifting that off, Alice beckoned to the Judge and the Band. There in a tiny, jug-shaped hollow in the turf about six inches deep, was a nest lined with soft white down plucked from over the little mother's throbbing heart. Inside were six little brown heads, six wriggly brown noses, six pairs of tightly closed little eyes, with a black line between them, and six pairs of flappy ears. Right out on the open turf, the mother rabbit had dug her nest and hidden her babies so carefully that not one of the children who had run past and over the nest scores of times had ever suspected that it was there, except Alice-Palace. Everyone had to come up and pat the little funny noses and tickle the soft waving ears. Then covering the opening again with the patch of rabbit wool and fitting back the leaves, they left the nest to Mrs. Bunny.

The Captain told them that she would guard it during the day, driving off cats or birds and leading dogs away from the place. As soon as it was dusk she would slip into the nest herself and feed and cuddle her brown babies all through the long night.

After this last nest, the Captain and the Judge had a long talk together while the Band waited anxiously for the decision. Finally, the Captain announced it.

"The Judge," he said, "is unable to decide which was the most interesting nest. As soon as she settles on one, she begins to remember another. It will be necessary either not to give any prize at all"—here the Captain made a long pause— "or," he resumed hurriedly, seeing the mouths of Alice-Palace and Henny-Penny opening for simultaneous howls, "to give a prize to each and every single solitary member of the Band. The philanthropist who offered the prize is a noble, generous-hearted man, almost too good for this world. I know him very well, indeed, and I feel sure that he will insist upon doing this."

All of which is the reason why every member of the Band is now armed with the latest thing in pocket cameras.

THE QUEEN FLOWER

Every year the night before the first of July the Captain always left the Band and travelled two hundred miles into the northern part of Connecticut. When he came back, he would say that he had seen the most beautiful thing in the world, but he would never tell what it was. This year, he took the Band with him. Late in the evening of the very last day of June, they all met in a house which their great-great grandfather had built. There, they had a wonderful supper and right afterwards went to bed. It seemed to them that they had hardly closed their eyes when they were awakened before daybreak by the Captain, who told them to dress quickly and quietly. The night hawks were still twanging in the dawn-dusk as they followed a dim, silent road which led over the hills and away, all sweet with the scent of wild grape and the drugged perfume of chestnut tassels. They crossed the bridge over the brook and the Captain showed them where he used to stand and catch chubs and minnows when he was about as old as Henny-Penny. He showed them, too, the very place by the Sheep Pool where once upon a time he had seen a monstrous milk snake crawl across the path into a hay field. He was so scared that he climbed up into an apple tree and stayed there until rescued by a searching party long after supper time. The Band were much pained at this instance of the lack of courage on the part of their Captain at the beginning of his career.

"You might have know that milk snakes aren't dangerous," said Trottie, patronizingly.

"Only to mice," agreed Honey, learnedly.

"Yes," said the Captain, "but I didn't have, like you, someone to tell me all those things, wise, kind, smart—"

"And boasty," finished Alice-Palace, which made all the Band, including the Captain, laugh very loud.

Finally, they reached the old farmhouse where the Captain's father had been born and where the Captain had spent all of his summers as a boy. In front was an enormous, wide, flat stepping stone which the Captain told them had been the hearth stone of his grandfather's first house. Then he showed them a deep gouge in the stone, which had been made nearly a hundred years ago by the axe of old black Hen, who had been brought from Africa as a cook on a trading schooner and lived all his life with the Captain's grandfather. He had a bad temper, and one night became so angry that he sunk his axe deep into the hearth stone and went off and was gone two years before he came back.

As they climbed the winding road which led up over the hill, the Captain showed them Hen's Pine on Pond Hill, which Hen had begged the wood choppers to spare when they cut down all the other trees. Under it was buried Hen's old horse Bill, and he had wanted to lie there himself with his axe, his fiddle, and the long whip with which he used to drive a four-in-hand on state occasions. Instead, he sleeps on a green hilltop beside his old master.

As they climbed farther and farther up the hill, the whole Band were anxious to know what they were going to see, but the Captain told them they must wait. Finally the road passed a forgotten barway so sunken in masses of sweet fern and so overshadowed by thickets of alder and witch hazel that it could hardly be seen. Here, the Captain stopped them.

"This is the gateway to the Land of Heart's Desire," he told them.

Then he parted the branches and led the way into the hush of the sleeping wood. Just beyond the open barway a moss-carpeted wood road began. They followed it for a time, until at last they came to some hidden mark that only the Captain knew. There, they turned off into the green tangle of a marshy thicket. Through masses of glossy Christmas ferns and clumps of feathery, tossing maidenhair, they crept in single file. Through the thick arched branches overhead, the dawn light filtered until the dusk around them became all green and gold. At last before them loomed up a squat, broken, white pine. This, the Captain told them, was the landmark for which he had been looking. Beyond, they pushed their way through a tangle of sanicle and the Captain stopped them in front of a slim elm in whose rough bark was carved a rude cross, which he told them he had cut to mark the place nearly ten years before.

"Now," he said in a hushed voice, "on the other side of this tree, if we are lucky, someone is waiting for us."

Close together they stepped out beyond the tree and caught a gleam of a white cross through the dusk. There, all rose red and snow white, with parted lips, waited for them the loveliest flower of their lives, that great orchid: the pink and white lady's slipper. It grew on a tall, round stem covered with fine down above brilliant green, curved leaves. The flower had two narrow, white curved petals, while at right angles towered one of the three sepals, making the snowy cross which they had first seen. Below the cross hung the lip of the flower, a milk-white, hollow shell fully an inch across and an inch deep and veined with crystalline pink, which deepened into purple. Inside were spots of intense purple which showed through the transparent walls. The other two white sepals were joined together and hung as one behind the lip, while inside the flower an ivory white and gold tongue, flecked with wine-colored spots, curved down into the shell. For long and long they looked before they said goodbye to the Queen.

"We'll come again and see you every year," called Henny-Penny, looking wistfully back as they started homewards at last through the tall ferns.

POND-LILY PATH

It had been too hot to work and almost too hot to play. Across the green lawn and against the pink dogwood tree, the little waves of heat quivered upward. One by one, the members of the Band took refuge under the cool shade of the great white oak tree just outside of the house. Even Henny-Penny and Alice-Palace, the twins, came panting back from some important secret mission and threw themselves down within the cool circle of shade.

"I wish," said Trottie, languidly, "that I was swimming in a nice, deep, cool pool. The water would be all goldy-brown and every once in a while, I would duck under and swim along the bottom. It would be covered with yellow and white sand, and I would pick up colored pebbles and mussel shells, all mother-of-pearl inside, and I would let the current carry me down and down, and I would stay in hours and hours."

"Huh," broke in the Third rudely, "you're talking about the Rancocas and the swimming pool by the

Cabin. It's too hot to get there, and the Captain wouldn't let you stay in hours and hours anyway."

Just at this psychological moment, a rapid fire volley of toots sounded from the lower gate. Before the astonished eyes of the Band, an extremely shiny car came speeding around the sharp turns of the steep road. It was Honey, sitting cross-legged on a low branch of the oak, who first recognized the driver.

"It's Fathy!" he squealed delightedly down to the rest.

Sure enough, the car sped tootingly forward, swung around the curve by the garage, and halted in front of the assembled Band. Such a loud shout went up that it awoke Mother, who had been sleeping in a cool hammock on the veranda.

"It suddenly occurred to me," the Captain explained, "that it was entirely too hot to practice law safely. Accordingly, absolutely regardless of expense, I have had put up the nicest, coldest lunch that money could buy. If I could possibly get any company," he went on reflectively, "I think I would run out to the Cabin and take a swim, and come back in the moonlight when it's cool. I suppose, though," he continued, "that you people are all too busy even to think of such a thing."

There was a rush and a scramble which lasted not over ten seconds. The eleventh found Henny-Penny and Alice-Palace in the front seat with the Captain, while Mother, the Third, Honey, and Trottie filled the back seat so tightly that it seemed hardly possible that any of them would ever be able to get out. In a minute, they were speeding along the thirty miles that separated them from the Cabin and the swimming hole so fast that a breeze blew into their faces in spite of the heat.

"It was me who did all this," triumphed Trottie. "I just wished for this with my wishing-stone and it came true."

Not even the Third contradicted him. Two hours later found the whole Band in the pool, carrying out the program of Trottie and his wishing-stone. They dived, they swam, they floated, and they splashed, and they ducked, and they laughed, and they squealed (especially Alice-Palace) for fully an hour in the magic water in which bare legs and arms turned a golden bronze. Finally, they came out and dressed and ate the lunch of which the Captain had boasted. It was just as good as he said it was.

In the cool of the afternoon, they started exploring. Down among the Pine Barrens where the Cabin stood, this was a favorite game. Everywhere, through the tangled scrub oaks and pitch pines, ran little paths. Some of them they had learned. There was the concealed path which led to Sam Carpenter's cranberry bog, which started at a little side door in his saw mill and wound through ostrich and interrupted ferns waist-high. It sometimes was so covered up that it could not be seen, but had to be felt out by the feet of the one going first. Then there was the winding wood road which led to the Upper Mill, five long miles away. The Captain had finally learned this, although twice he lost himself and wandered a whole day through a maze of paths and endless stretches of barrens before he found his way back.

Today, they started on the narrow path which led to Annie's Bog, less than two miles away. As they started along the winding path which the Captain had cut through the thickets from the main road to the Cabin, he slipped on ahead. As the Band turned around a sharp curve, suddenly, an enormous animal rushed on all fours at them from a withewood thicket with fearsome roarings and loud and terrifying growly noises. In the narrow pathway, the whole Band fell backward over each other while the cautious Honey, who was bringing up the rear, fled for his life and did not stop until he was safe again on the Cabin porch, ready to repel bears and other dangerous boarders. It turned out, after all, to be only the Captain, whereupon the whole Band fell upon him and rolled over and over among the prickly scrub oak leaves until he begged for mercy.

As they came to the main road, Trottie was seized with a brilliant idea. He would scurry around the bend and hide himself and spring out at the Captain. Accordingly, he slipped unobtrusively away. The next thing the Band knew, they heard from the nearby woods the voice of Trottie on high.

"Ow! ow!" he shouted, and in a minute there was a crackle in the underbrush and down and through the bushes he burst, still making the same remark at the very top of his voice.

His round face was all puckered up with pain, and with every jump he yelled "Ow! ow!" as loud as any ten year old boy could possibly be expected to yell. The Captain ran forward, but Trottie was too far gone for words. He finally managed to point to one bare leg, and there, sure enough, was a cluster of no less than six big black-and-white hornets, each one stinging away with all its might. The Captain had no more than brushed these off when Trottie pointed to another place. Both legs, one arm, and one cheek were badly stung, and, in spite of his advanced age and the honorable position of second lieutenant which he had won in the Band, he cried aloud before them all under the intolerable smart of the stings. The Captain did not waste a moment. Running down the road he came back with a handful of bluish-purple flowers growing in a spike and with long curved leaves.

"Quick," he said, "chew this," and he poked a bundle of hurriedly plucked leaves into Trottie's mouth just in time to stop another cry.

Trottie did as he was told, and the Captain placed a hurried poultice of the chewed leaves on each sting. Almost as if by magic, the pain stopped, and a wan smile appeared on Trottie's tearful face.

"Gee," he remarked, "that feels good. What is it?"

"That," said the Captain, "is 'heal-all.' It's guaranteed to cure all aches, pains, stings or burns, even such severe wounds as our brave comrade sustained."

"He cried some," said Henny-Penny, "that wasn't very brave."

"Well," said the Captain, "it wouldn't be ordinarily, but eleven hornets all at once entitle any one to a reasonable amount of cry."

The Band turned off to a road which cut in at an acute angle. They followed this for a few rods. Suddenly, it disappeared. At right angles to its end, a dim path showed through the blueberry bushes, which wound in and out in a delightfully mysterious, puzzling way and constantly crossed and recrossed by other paths, which no one had ever had time to follow out to the end.

"It's just like the paths in 'The Cloister and the Hearth,'" observed the Third delightedly.

"Yes," chimed in Trottie, forgetting his aches, "that place where Girard and Martin take her hand and run with the bloodhounds after them."

"There aren't not any bad old bloodhounds here, are there, Fathy?" inquired Henny-Penny anxiously, closing up quite close to the Captain.

"Oo-oo-boo-oo," barked the teasing Trottie from behind a bush in what he fondly believed was the very best brand of bloodhound bark.

The startled and irate Henny-Penny, however, at once detected the imposture and pursued Second-Lieutenant Trottie with a sharp stick. Trottie was only saved from punishment for his attempt to trifle with Henny-Penny's feelings by a shout from Honey, who had been carefully observing the sides of the path.

Over there among the blueberry bushes and the sweet fern, he had spied a beautiful flower swinging in mid-air like a purple-pink butterfly. The flower grew from two narrow leaves almost like the narrow-leafed plantain. There were five beautiful petals arranged something like a fleur de lis, with two extra petals added at the base. At either side of the glorious figure curled a long, pink tongue, one of them being surrounded by a fuzz of golden anthers. It was the calopogon, or grass pink, one of the most beautiful of the summer orchids.

A moment later, Henny-Penny found a glorious towering lily with curled back petals, which the Captain said was the celebrated Turk's cap lily. It was Mother who plunged into the woods suddenly and came back with a bough of sweet magnolia, with its glossy leaves and creamy white blossoms, which had a fragrance as overpowering as the scent of the tuberose.

Then the Third found a clump of sundews, those curious carnivorous plants with tiny white blossoms and round red leaves covered with reddish hairs, specked with little drops of sweet dew, which prove the death of many a passing insect. The wanderer alights to taste. Immediately, the hairs spring around him like a trap, and there he is held while the plant slowly drains his life blood.

This last find was too much for Alice-Palace. At first she had claimed that it was owing to her shortness that she had not seen the purple-pink orchid. She had been just on the point of finding both the magnolia and the lily when others, more greedy and grasping, had stepped in ahead of her. As for the sundews, she would have none of them.

"I wouldn't not want to find any old flower that kills nice buzzy little flies," she said scornfully. "I'm going to find a norful nice flower, much nicer than Henny-Penny's," she finished.

Thereupon she commenced to search, wearing her pout face, which was a sure sign that her feelings were much overwrought. A few minutes later, she was not there. Mother was the first one to notice her absence. The Captain looked a little worried.

"Don't any of you leave this path," he said, "except myself. Ten yards away and you'll all get lost. Probably she's gone on ahead."

Then he sent the Third to sprint on down the path as far as Annie's house, while he himself searched and called all through the adjoining barrens. Half an hour passed. The Third had come back with the word that there was no trace of Alice. The sun was getting low down in the sky. Mother looked as if she were going to cry.

"She's so little," she said to the Captain, and he made no reply except to dash out again in a wide circle through all the thickets and the interminable little groves of stunted pines which stretched for miles and miles, all looking exactly alike. Finally, he came back.

"Now," he said, "let's all call her name together as loud as we can ten times with a wait between each call."

So, they started with a shout that made the empty woods echo far and near. Then they waited, but there was only the call of the chewink as he sung for the thousandth time: "Come to me-e-e-e, come to me, come to me," while the gay little note of the Maryland yellowthroat, with his black mask and tilted tail, seemed to mock and flout them as he sang, "Wichita, wichita, wichita." Again they shouted and again they waited. For a third time they gave a call, which seemed to have something of a hopeless drag to it, and Henny-Penny, her twin, cried so that he could call no more.

"I wisht I had let her find my lily," he wailed.

His crying was contagious, and the next call was made all alone by the Captain, and his voice quavered a good deal at the finish. The echoes, however, had hardly died out before someone suddenly said, "Here I am," and there from out a little half-concealed path that no one had thought of following bobbed the missing Alice-Palace.

They were all too glad to scold her. Moreover, she was too swelling with importance to be reproved or even petted.

"Come, Fathy," she said, "I want to show you sompin'. All the rest can come, too," she called back condescendingly as she pulled him down the hidden path.

For a while, it ran almost straight between rows of pine trees and then it took a sudden turn and was out in the Barrens, where there was nothing except patches of white sand. Here and there, it wound, twisting and turning like a snake. Now, it crossed a deep little ditch and reappeared near the side. Once, it skirted the edge of a marshy place, but finally, it stretched straight and clear across what looked like the moors of old England about which the children had so often read.

For half a mile, the Band trotted after Alice. Suddenly, the path turned and ran along the side of what looked like a great dike. Some forgotten cranberry grower had once started to drain a faraway bog and had dug a ditch clear into the dry barrens. The water had followed the ditch and then had made a little course of its own beside the long bank.

Alice ran on ahead and beckoned the Band to look. Down below them stretched a still, brown brook with a hardly perceptible current. In its dark depths floated scores and scores of great white fragrant flowers with golden hearts, the rare white pond lily, which no one had ever known grew in that part of the Barrens.

"I told you," said Alice, as they came back fifteen minutes later with great sheaths of the fragrant flower, "that my flower'd be bettern any."

And no one contradicted her.

SHEEP-PEN HILL

The Band was out exploring. The Captain had a large pair of field glasses guaranteed to show the pink beak of a field sparrow at a hundred yards. Henny-Penny was armed with a high-powered, repeating trowel for digging up ferns, flowers, plants, trees—anything which might, could, would, or should grow in his wildflower garden, and wore a dark smouch on the very end of his nose. Alice-Palace carried a basket nearly as big as herself, the which was intended to hold all of Henny-Penny's loot, as well as any animal, vegetable, or mineral bric-a-brac she might acquire herself. The Third had an imposing notebook and a shiny yellow pencil. Trottie and Honey took turns in carrying what was probably the finest exploratory lunch that had been put up since Balboa discovered the Pacific. Altogether, Vasco da Gama, De Soto, Magellan, or any other professional explorer might have been proud to head such a well-equipped band of adventurers.

On the way to Annie's Bog, Henny-Penny noticed a strange brown spot on Alice-Palace's forehead. On close inspection he was horrified to find that said spot was really a flat, many-legged bug with a long, sharp beak that was buried in Alice-Palace's white skin. The Captain had to be called before that fierce bug could be dislodged. He told them that it was a wood tick.

"You can hear a watch tick and see a bedtick, but not a wood tick," he assured them solemnly.

Soon after the repulse of the tick attack the Band came to a place where a maze of paths crossed the one which they were following.

"Comrades," announced the Captain, "the secret of all successful exploring is to follow your nose," whereupon he plunged into the faintest path of all, one nearly hidden in a tangle of sweetfern.

In and out, it ran for miles over bare white sand, through clumps of feathery Hudsonia and among masses of sandmyrtle with its shining, oval, dark green leaves. Suddenly, another path from nowhere cut across at right angles. Unhesitatingly, the Captain turned into it followed by the Band. Straight westwards, the path ran in the direction which explorers have taken since time began, following the side of a long straight ditch dug generations ago by some forgotten cranberry grower. In the distance was a dark cedar swamp where gaunt skeleton trees showed here and there in pools of black water. The Band closed up close to the Captain. Anything might dwell there—slimy dragons, smooth, sly water snakes, monsters of all sorts. Suddenly, the Captain stopped. Just beyond a tangled thicket the brook made a bend and there in a sort of pocket were a few rods of level green marsh. The waving green was stained here and there with strange, beautiful flowers that looked as though a swarm of pink butterflies had alighted for a moment on the grass-tops. The flowers themselves grew on long green stems like blades of grass and ended in tiny white bulbs. These stems were in angled joints and from each bend sprang a blossom about an inch long which had five petals of a purple-pink deepening at the center to a pink-purple. Above them towered a heart-shaped lip bearing a brush of orange, rose, and yellow bristles. For long, the Band looked and looked. Henny-Penny's trowel twitched in his hand but the Captain told him that the flowers would not transplant.

"The darlingest things I ever saw," cried Alice-Palace, stretching out her arms toward them.

The Captain said that it was a colony of the grass pink, one of the most beautiful of our orchids. One only was picked to show Mother, for to pick an orchid means that the flower will not come up again. While the Third was making extensive notes for the "Band-Book," from out of the marsh ahead a great bird flapped. It had such vast wings that Alice-Palace was positive that it was a Roc. The Captain said that although it did have a Roc-ish look it was really a great blue heron, the largest bird in Eastern America.

Just after this, they came to a couple of maple poles stretched across the brook, which must have been there for a long, long time, since the bark had all rotted off from them both. Testing them carefully, the Captain teetered his way over. Then from the other side, he stretched a long stick. With that as a support, beginning with the littlest, one by one, the rest of the Band sidled across—all except Second-Lieutenant Trottie. That gallant officer scorned any help. At first, he had no trouble with the tippy bridge. Then the wretched poles began to sway. Trottie balanced desperately like a rope dancer, but when one pole turned completely over he stepped into the deep brown water with a howl. Thereafter, he crawled dripping up the bank amid great laughter. The Captain told him that he was proud of his bravery—but not of his sense, which made the Band laugh more than ever.

Just beyond the poles the Captain began to search through the long marsh grass.

"Hist!" he said at last mysteriously and disappeared among the bushes. When the Band reached the place, they found the beginning of a path deep trodden in the grass and cut through the very heart of dense thickets. Sometimes it was so covered by fern and brake that they could only follow it by feeling it underfoot. For miles and miles, it wound over hillocks and through bogs. Then, it disappeared and the Band found themselves on a narrow road crossing a wide, flat stretch of grassy land. Beyond a clump of trees, they stepped suddenly into a little village. There was a public square with a wooden pump; a store, an inn and some twenty houses were scattered along two or three short streets. The Band marched down the main road expecting every minute to meet someone or to hear voices, but there was no sight nor sound. Then, a chewink sang from the porch of the store and the shy prairie warbler ran up its scale of six notes near a boarded window. The leaves lay thick on the house steps and there weren't any wheel marks or footprints on the streets. The Captain told them that this must be the deserted settlement of Sheep Pen Hill, to which he had never been able to find his way before. Fifty years ago, a hundred people lived there and raised sheep in fields, which had long gone back to brush and blueberries.

For a while, the Band wandered among the empty houses. Then, suddenly, they all decided at the same time that they wanted to go home. Why did the old houses stare at them so? Why had men deserted the place? Hurrying back on their tracks, they stole away, nor did they feel quite easy again until a high ridge hid the gaunt, staring houses from their sight. In the depths of a wood all sweet with the scent of white azalea and the spicy fragrance of magnolia and bayberry, they spent so much time on that wonderful lunch that the sun was set before they reached the Cabin and Mother.

THE PLAINS

The Captain had just come back from the hot city to the Cabin, set in a fringe of cool green boughs. From beside the leaning pine that marked the deepest part of the Pool he dived straight and deep. Swimming under the cedar water that turned his bare arms and legs all gold he stayed down so long that the pessimistic Henny-Penny feared the worst. Then suddenly he was on the top of the Pool, giving a wonderful exhibition of all the swimming strokes known to man. At least so he said. Then he went under again and swam down with the current clear to the white sand beach around the bend. There he floated and ate blueberries from the laden overhanging bushes. The Band could only envy him from the bank, since each one had already equaled the Cabin's allowance of three swims per day. Finally, when he came out and was dry and dressed and cool, he assembled the Band. To them he spoke with the stern brevity which characterizes all great leaders.

"Tomorrow afternoon, two thirty-five, tank duty."

At exactly 2:34½ P. M. the next day, shortly after the arrival of the afternoon train from the city, there sounded in the sandy road outside the woods in which the Cabin was buried a puffing and a rumbling and a clanking which made the Band squeal like anything. When, however, they charged at full speed into the road from out the winding path they found that the tank was only the station agent's big motortruck, all fitted up with seats and big enough to hold Band and baggage. In exactly eleven seconds, suntime, they were all at their stations, prepared for anything. The Captain said that if they would only be as prompt for breakfast duty and bed duty it would make his life far happier. Then as they went rumbling and rattling and lurching along he told them that they were bound for the Plains. This was a stretch of thirty square miles of plateau, set in the wildest and most inaccessible part of the Barrens, where nothing grew over two feet high. All the trees were dwarfed, like the funny tiny ones in Japanese tea gardens.

"What makes 'em so littly?" inquired Henny-Penny, the gardener.

"That," replied the Captain, "is a secret which I mustn't tell."

"He won't tell because he doesn't know," called out Mother from the front seat. The Captain said if he heard any more such talk someone would be court-martialed, which made the Band laugh, for of course a Captain couldn't court-martial a General.

Before long the narrow road became even narrower, and ran through dense thickets and dark cedar swamps, where the tank cut its way through overhanging boughs. In places the Band had to lie down flat on their tummies not to be slashed by the whipping branches through which they crashed. Once they came out into a long, grassy stretch where a mansion house was mouldering away in the woods where great glassworks used to stand. Later they passed ironworks abandoned for half a hundred years. Where there used to be the hum and roar of furnaces, now there was nothing but the singing of the wind through the low pine trees. The Captain told them that this was Mary Ann's Forge, where many of the cannon which the Continental Army used in the Revolution had been made out of bog iron. The owner had named it after his favorite daughter.

"I'm going to call it the Alice-Palace Forge," announced the Corporal of the Band. "It's a *much* prettier name."

Thereupon arose a discussion which lasted for at least five miles between the Corporal and the Sergeant, who felt strongly that the place should be christened "Henny-Penny Forge."

At last after hours' traveling through a maze of intersecting, twisting, half-hidden roads the tank began to climb toward a distant ridge of trees.

"Everyone shut their eyes tight," commanded the Captain, "until I give the word to look."

Accordingly the whole Band, including the Captain and the Quartermaster General, sat silent with eyes screwed tight shut. Only the driver kept his open. Anyway, he had been there before, so that it did not matter. At last the Band felt the tank pass over the ridge and down on the other side.

"Open Sesame!" shouted the Captain, quite like Ali Baba. There was a chorus of Oh's from everyone. Before them stretched a vast, rolling plain, sparsely covered with what looked to be low bushes, but which were really tiny trees. Everywhere were blueberries, and the Band did very little investigation until they had consumed a quart or so apiece of these. Then the Captain called them to see a strange plant. It looked like a clump of dead leaves and stalks, out of which were growing scores and hundreds of tiny green stems with pinkish, purplish ends looking almost like pine needles. He told them that this was the celebrated Conrade's crowberry which had been discovered nearly a hundred years ago by a man named Conrade at Pemberton. Then it had been lost for fifty years, only to be found again in the Plains.

"Is it good to eat?" demanded the unbotanical Alice-Palace.

"No, but it's very interesting," explained the Captain.

"Not to me," responded the Corporal, returning to her blueberry patch.

It was Trottie who made the discovery of the day. As he wandered through the knee-high forest, he heard in front of him a shrill peeping like that of little chickens, except for a curious little upward trill at the end of every peep. He called the Captain. Hunt as they would, they could not catch a glimpse of the peepers, but the Captain said that he had heard the same in the barrens of the island of Martha's Vineyard, and that he believed they had come upon a brood of young heath hens. The heath hen is the Eastern form of the prairie chicken, which two hundred years ago used to be found all through the Eastern states. Today it is supposed to be entirely extinct except in certain wild places on Martha's Vineyard. The Captain said that he would arrange to have the Band visit the Plains again in the spring. Then if there were any heath hens living there, they would hear the strange, booming sound which the cocks make from two yellow air sacs set on either side of their necks.

As the light at the edge of the Plains began to turn purple and the shadows of the little trees grew longer and longer, the Band sat down to supper. Across the ridges and up and down the hollows swept a cool salt breeze from the ocean miles away, and some way the Band felt sorry to leave the high still Plains and go down to everyday life again.

The most exciting adventure of the day came last. In the end of the twilight they were whirling through the woods, when suddenly up from the brush, not fifty yards away, sprang two lithe, beautiful, red-brown deer. One was a buck with a magnificent pair of branching antlers. He was in such a hurry to get away that he tripped and fell to his knees, while his mate, a wide-eyed doe, stopped and waited for him. Then they both started off again at full speed only to stop once more to look at the strange, puffing, rattling thing which had roused them from their thicket. For long human folk and wild folk stared at each other through the trees, and the Band's last memory of that day was their wild, beautiful faces.

THE HUNTING OF THE SWIFT

"An' then, an' then!" went on Alice-Palace, "a great big norful Swift came and ate up the big old, bad old boy, but it never touched the neatly, tidy little girl."

"Pooh," said the disorderly Henny-Penny uneasily, "I'd whisk up a tree and the old Swift'd never catch me."

"Swifts can climb like anything," responded Alice-Palace.

"They can't," bellowed her twin.

"They can," shrilled Alice-Palace, and the dispute was taken to the Captain.

"Both of you are right," was his diplomatic decision. "It all depends on the swift. Chimney Swifts can't climb, Pine Swifts can."

"What kind of a bird is a Pine Swift?" inquired Trottie, the ornithologist of the band.

The Captain pondered deeply. "Comrades," he announced suddenly, "at daybreak tomorrow we start to hunt the Pine Swift to his lair. To bed at once; you'll need all your strength." And the Captain shook his head ominously.

That very night each member of the Band prepared for the worst. Honey put new rubbers on his trusty sling-shot, with which he could frequently hit a barn door at five paces. Trottie oiled up the air rifle, which he was only allowed to use in windowless wildernesses. Henny-Penny kept up such a fusillade with his new popgun that mother threatened to send him forth unarmed on the morrow if she heard but one more pop. Alice-Palace's practice, however, was the most spectacular. She had a water pistol, which when properly charged would propel a stream of water an unbelievable distance. From the bathroom door she took a snapshot at Henny-Penny, who was approaching her confidingly. The charge took effect in the very center of a large pink ear. It was a long time before Henny-Penny could be convinced that he was not mortally wounded.

At dawn the next morning from the Captain's room sounded the adventure call of the Band. Followed thumps, splashings, and sounds of rapid dressing from the third story, where the Band bivouacked.

Noon found them miles deep in the Barrens. On every side stretched miles and miles and miles of stiff green pitch pines like trees for a Noah's ark, all overhung by a warm blue sky. Far, far overhead wheeled and swung a great black bird with fringed wings. Beyond him was another and still another, and way off by the horizon was a black speck which the Captain said was yet another. He told them that these were turkey buzzards, or vultures, wheeling back and forth and quartering the whole sky watching for any dying or dead animal. If one vulture dropped down to earth he would be followed by the next and the next, like a long chain, until six or eight buzzards would gather around the carcass. Then the Captain told them how the buzzard nests in hollow logs in the barrens, and what an exciting thing it is to find a nest, because a nesting buzzard has a dangerous habit. He wouldn't tell them what the habit was, though they guessed and guessed.

All along the pathways grew clumps of low bushes covered with bright golden blossoms, which the wind piled up in little yellow drifts against the white sand. This was the Hudsonia or barrens heather, the Captain said, and a new lot of blossoms bloomed on each plant every day to make up for those which the wind blew away. Suddenly from out of a leucothoe bush all covered with swinging fragrant white bells a little bird with an olive back, a saucy tilted tail, a yellow throat and breast, and a black mask over its cheeks and eyes, sang and sang and sang.

"It says, 'What-a-pity, what-a-pity, what-a-pity,'" said Alice-Palace.

The Captain told the Band that it was the Maryland or northern yellowthroat, one of the warblers that lived in the Barrens. As they came near the bird stopped singing and was joined by the female, who had the olive back and yellow throat, but lacked the mask. Then they met a pair of chewinks, black and white over rust-red, which began to dive through the bushes and call out, "Chit! Chit! Chit!" as sharply as if they had pebbles in their throats. That meant, the Captain told them, that there was a nest on the ground somewhere near.

So the whole Band began to hunt and hunt. It was like playing "hot and cold," for when they got near the nest the birds would flutter around frantically and redouble their alarm notes. If they moved away, the birds became quieter. Finally, Henny-Penny happened to look at the foot of a little clump of sheep laurel all full of deep pink flowers, and there was the nest, all made of pine needles. The four eggs were speckled all over with brownish-red marks. The Band all crowded around to look and the Captain made Alice-Palace and Henny-Penny keep their hands behind their backs for fear they would touch the eggs and perhaps make the mother bird desert the nest. They all looked and looked until they had learned the birds and the nest and the eggs so that they would never forget them. The Captain told them that was the best way to collect eggs, always to leave them in the nest and study them there. Then their collection wouldn't be spoiled by any memories of fluttering, crying mother birds, mourning their lost eggs and ruined nests.

When at last they left the nest it was lunch time, and they all started for the Cabin, which overhung a bank of the crooked brown Rancocas Creek. As they trooped hungrily in at the door they heard a loud, deep hum, which seemed to come from all parts of the room at once. Just over the dining table hung from the rafter a swaying, golden-brown, seething, humming mass of bees about the size and shape of a long watermelon. It was a runaway swarm from some hive, which had come down the chimney. The Captain told them that if the swarm were not touched it would do them no harm. A broken swarm, however, he said, was dangerous. Men and animals have been stung to death by accidentally running against one. So they all sat and ate and ate very quietly. Even Alice-Palace talked in whispers, her eyes fixed on the swaying swarm above. At last the Captain announced that all world records for long-distance eating were broken. Anyway, everything was gone. So they stopped. Just then something squeaked and chattered from the small fireplace at the opposite side of the room. Trottie ran over to see.

"Come quick!" he shouted. "Here's two weeny little birds on a funny nest." The Band rushed to him.

As they got there a rumbling noise like thunder came from the chimney, which made the cautious Henny-Penny retire behind the Captain with wonderful rapidity. The Captain told them that the nest was that of a chimney swift which had fallen, and that the noise was made by the beating of the swifts' wings as they flew out of the chimney.

The nest itself was made of little sticks all glued together and fastened to the chimney. The Captain told them that the swifts break off these dead twigs from the trees while in full flight and glue them with a sticky liquid from their bills. The two naked little birds cried and cried, but the Captain set them and the nest up in a ledge inside the chimney so that after the Band had gone the mother bird might come back and feed them.

Then he took the Band outside and in the high sky showed them birds with cigar-shaped bodies circling and twittering far above. These were chimney-swifts, and he showed them how they could be told from swallows by their differently shaped bodies and by their flight. The wings of a swift flutter alternately, while those of a swallow for the most part swoop together.

Then they marched in single file through the pine trees, keeping a very close watch on every side for the other swifts. Suddenly right ahead of Henny-Penny something shot across the hot sand, over the dry leaves and up a tree before he could even pop once. The Band halted with raised weapons.

"What was that?" inquired Honey tremulously.

"That," said the Captain, peering up the tree, "was a Swift."

"It looked more like a Streak," remarked Trottie.

Just then a gray-ridged head looked around the tree trunk about ten feet up. Instantly there sped unerringly (more or less) toward said head a devastating volley, to wit, one buckshot, one pebble, one stream of water and no fewer than four exceedingly loud pops. The fiercest Swift could not stand against such a fusillade. This one did not even try. The head disappeared in a wink. Just as the Band believed the Swift to be fatally wounded it peeped out from the other side of the tree. Then in a flash it was staring at them from behind a branch, from back of a stub, from down near the foot of the tree, from up at the tiptop. There was no place where that unscrupulous Swift might not be expected. Only when all the ammunition was gone did the Captain enter the fray with a long stick. By this time the Swift was back in his original position, his sly head peering down at them. The Captain executed a flank movement. While the Swift was waiting ready to dodge a frontal attack, he was suddenly dislodged by a well-directed poke from the rear. As he struck the ground the whole Band pounced on him. Close at hand the Swift did not seem very fierce after all. He was only a spiny little lizard with a long, wriggly tail, a gray, black-banded back and bright blue blotches along the lower part of his sides. He was passed from hand to hand. Henny-Penny gloated over him.

"I bet it was my popgun that scared this old Swift down," he bragged.

Just then a startling thing happened. Henny-Penny had loosened his grip during his boasty talk. Suddenly the Swift flashed out of his hand, up his arm and disappeared down his neck. Up and down Henny-Penny's bare back and around and across his round tummy and up and down his waving arms raced the Swift. As the scaly, spiny little body ran up and down his bare skin, Henny-Penny went nearly frantic. The rest of the Band danced around trying to help. Finally, just as Henny-Penny was desperately tearing off his shirt, the wretched Swift flashed into view again, this time out of one of the legs of his knickerbockers, and disappeared under a bush.

"I told you Swifts could climb," exulted Alice-Palace.

THE ARGONAUTS

And they rowed away over the wine-dark sea, heroes all,
beyond the sunset where were gold, monsters, enchanted
islands, and strange peoples. For some death waited. For
all a fame which still rings across the vanished years.

No one spoke for a long minute as the Captain finished reading to the Band before bedtime a chapter from the story of that Voyage after the Golden Fleece when the world was young.

"There aren't any more quests left now," said Trottie at last, wistfully. "Everything's been found,—even the North Pole. There's only school and games and books and growing up and working and getting old. Why can't we have adventures nowadays?"

"We can!" shouted the Captain suddenly. "Everybody can. The world is full of wonderful adventures for those who look for them. Nobody needs to grow old. Just you wait until Saturday and we'll go argonauting; Mother and all."

The end of the week found the whole Band on the bank of the Rancocas, which came running swiftly and silently to meet them from the depths of the pine barrens. In front of the cabin, tied to a white cedar, was something the sight of which made the Band shout like anything. There, rocking in the golden water, was the largest, shiniest, beautifulest canoe that ever a band went adventuring in. Along its green side in crimson letters was painted—"The Argo."

In less than one minute by the cabin clock every one of the Band was safely stored aboard except Mother. She had charge of the commissary, and said that she would stay behind and arrange for the feast that all rightminded Argonauts expect when they bring back a golden fleece. Even without her it was a pretty close fit. On the rear seat was the Captain, with the biggest paddle in captivity. Sandwiched in between the next two thwarts, on the bottom of the canoe, sat Alice-Palace and Henny-Penny, pledged not to move whatever happened. Trottie and Honey-Bee, disagreeing about something, as usual, were wedged in beyond, while the Third paddled bow. A few strokes took them out of the pool. The Cabin disappeared around a sharp bend. The quest had begun.

Sing, O Muse, of the perils by sea and land endured by that dauntless crew. First came "Sunken Log," a bare two inches under the whirling water except at one end, where there was a passage if the canoe were jammed into a tangle of cranberry vines on the bank and swung into the current at just the right instant. The Captain said afterward that it was the Third's fault, and the Third was positive that the Captain was to blame. Anyway, the Argo scraped, and for a perilous instant stuck. In another second she would have swung broadside to the swift current and capsized. Only a tremendous burst of paddling, aided by loud squeals from Alice-Palace and Henny-Penny, saved the day. Just in time she slid squeakingly into safety.

Followed a long stretch, where the crooning water ran under star-leaved sweet gums, while the banks were fringed with pitcher plants, cassandra, sweet pepper-bush and carpeted with wine-colored pyxie moss and yellow asters. Just beyond the bow of the Argo a red squirrel ran down the hanging branches and leaped across, clinging with his bent forepaws and swinging back and forth over the water like a pendulum. Painted terrapin scuttled off from sunken snags, and chewinks with rust-red sides scuffled among the leaves like little hens. Once the Watchman of the Creek, a big blue-gray and white kingfisher, flew ahead of the Argo, giving his warning rattle. Then came a place where the water was swift again and a tree-trunk stretched nearly across the stream, leaving a place little more than a yard wide through which the canoe must pass. It was a wonderful bit of steering. The Captain said so himself. The Argonauts at once named the place "Passage Perilous" from the *Morte d'Arthur*. Then there was the "Portcullis," where they passed under an overhanging tree with one long sharp branch hanging above the channel ready to scrape off any unwary voyager.

"Just like Scylla," said Honey, who had been dipping into the *Odyssey*. There did that hero, Henny-Penny, endure a woe almost too grievous to be borne, for from his very head did the dire Portcullis snatch a hat of great price with a beautiful roley brim, such as an Argonaut might be proud to wear. Then did Henny-Penny weep aloud for his loss bitter to be borne. Nor could the swift Argo stop in the midst of the stream. Then it chanced that as the current whirled the hat away it caught upon the branch of a sunken tree and hung safe and dry above the water. Whereupon the Captain cheered the hero, Henny-Penny, with winged words and the promise to restore the hat to him on the homeward voyage, so that his heart was comforted and he ceased from tears.

Beyond the scene of this happening, which I have tried to set forth in Homeric phrase, came the "Crooked S's," where the Rancocas doubled on itself again and again in such sharp curves that the canoe bumped from bank to bank a dozen times until the maze was passed. Farther on was the Speedway, where for a hundred yards the stream ran straight and swift. The green banks passed like the film of a moving picture, and the water swirled in ripples and coils of tawny gold under the quick paddle strokes. Just as it seemed as if the Argo were about to be dashed into a thicket of greenbrier the Captain executed a right-angle turn much applauded by the crew.

Mile after mile into unknown depths the voyage stretched on. There were no longer paths on the banks.

Anything, the Band felt, might lurk in the dark thickets past which they whirled. In fact, once, as they rounded a sudden curve, a lithe, brown, short-legged animal flashed into the tangled bushes with a snarl and a gleam of white teeth. The Captain said it was a mink—but the Band had their own private opinion. Then there was the Dragon. Said Dragon was draped across the tops of some sunken bushes by a still part of the stream. To be sure, he apparently fled under the water as they approached with dreadful swiftness, but the Band felt that this might be only a crafty plot on his part to catch them unawares. The Captain said it was a banded water snake, which, although bitey, was not venomous. Only the grim timber rattlesnake, the king of the forest, and the copperhead were dangerous in the northern states, he said. The Band knew better. Dragons are always venomous.

Finally the current became slower and the stream wider as it ran through a little marsh ringed around with woods. Suddenly in a ferny swale just beyond the wet bank Trottie's sharp eyes caught a gleam in the green grass.

"The Golden Fleece!" he shouted, and at the sight the Captain swung the Argo into harbor. The crew rushed ashore and fell on their knees before a mass of crested orange-gold spires, each one formed of scores and scores of tiny fringed flowers all set on a central stem. Petals, sepals, lips and fringed tongues all were a mass of burnished gold. It was a colony of the yellow-fringed orchids, so rare that not even the Captain had ever seen the flower before. Beyond, as far as they could see, the meadow was all a-gold. There were so many that each of the Band picked a great bunch to bring back to Mother, although usually orchids are to be seen but not picked, and as they journeyed back a host of slender golden wands waved goodby to them through the green depths of the marsh.

For the homeward voyage, Honey-Bee took the place of the Third at the bow. With the full speed of the current behind it, the good ship Argo rushed down stream. There was little time to hesitate at any of the hazards. Down the Speedway the canoe leaped like a salmon. Just in time the Captain remembered at which end of the log lay Hidden Passage. With one accord the heroes fell flat on their faces and whizzed under the Portcullis and leaped over Sunken Log without scathe. There, however, a couple of withe-wood boughs cut the bow paddler across the face like the slash of a whip. He had just opened his mouth for a cry that would have been heard clear to the Cabin when the Argo came to the Turn where a swirl of swift current set into the bare bole of a pitch pine. It was necessary to swing the bow of the canoe instantly out of the eddy into the quiet water beyond. The Captain backed and held the canoe with all his strength for a second against the current.

"Paddle!" he shouted. "You can cry later on."

Honey saw the force of this suggestion and paddled desperately to get the nose of the canoe about in time. It was a sharp bit of work, but he did it.

"Now, you can cry," said the Captain kindly as they swung into the smooth water.

"No," said Honey with much dignity. "It's too late now."

A little farther on, with a quick flip of his paddle the Captain rescued the precious headgear of Henny-Penny. Then came the Needle's Eye—and the canoe rushed down the current like a racehorse. The bow shot through safely, but the steersman waited a second too long and with his paddle cramped was swung against the jagged edge of the log. A quick writhe saved his skin but not his shirt. This was the last accident of the voyage and the Argo rounded the curve and came to rest in the Pool amid pæans of victory from the returning heroes.

At the Cabin Mother and the Banquet awaited them—both unsurpassed. The table, a Sheraton found by the Captain in an old, old house in the Barrens, was decorated with the honey-sweet blossoms of the white alder and strewn with gray-green bayberry leaves, golden asters, and purple boneset. The first course was served in cups of white oak leaves pinned together with thorns and filled with ripe, sweet blueberries. Then there came a green russula salad made of crisp, grayish-green mushrooms served raw, with French dressing, and crackers and cheese. There was fresh butter, cool and dewy from the refrigerator scooped out of a clay bank under the cold waters of the creek, and raisin and nut bread. Then came a wonderful catfish and eel fry, the results of two hours of fishing in the dark the night before by the Captain down by Lower Mill.

For dessert were baskets of New Jersey peaches picked that morning from a nearby peach orchard. In the middle of the table from a copper luster jug bought at another old house gleamed the golden trophy of the voyage. Each hero of the crew told Mother of the adventures of the voyage at length, and the feast stretched so far into the afternoon that the moon was rising over Violet Hill when the Band came home again.

TURTLE DAY

The Captain was coming home. You could tell that because the members of the Band, Brownie the dog, and Puffly the big Angora cat, were all running and rolling and tumbling down Violet Hill, which led to the gate. He had been away for a day and a night on a private exploring expedition by himself through the southern part of New Jersey. From the pockets of his shooting jacket sprays of sweet pink azalea showed, together with bunches of the blue bird's foot violet, with its dark clouded center, and wine-red pyxie moss starred with tiny white blossoms.

It was Trottie who made the first discovery.

"Ouch!" he remarked earnestly after slipping his hand into one of the many pockets of the shooting jacket. "There's something crawly there."

"It won't hurt you," reassured the Captain.

Trottie tried again and brought out a little round turtle with a black back bordered by twenty-five irregularly-shaped lozenges of shell. Inside of this border were eleven larger sections and down the middle of the back were three larger lozenges yet, all made by crisscross lines in the shell.

"The top of this turtle," lectured the Captain, "is called the 'carapace' and the under shell, which looks like a piece of pinky-brown soap, is the 'plastron.' You see how smooth it is. That shows this turtle likes a sandy brook; otherwise, the plastron would be scratched and cut from crawling over stones. The name of the owner of said carapace and plastron," he went on, "is Painted Turtle, and you see he is just about as big around as the palm of my hand."

"Why is it called 'painted'?" inquired Honey, who always wanted to know.

"Look," said the Captain, turning the turtle over. The under edge of the shell was beautifully mottled all the way round in vivid red and black.

"Does he bite?" inquired Alice-Palace anxiously.

"No," responded the Captain, pulling out the reluctant little head with its beautiful black and gold eyes, and showing her the tiny black claws on each foot and the red and black tail tucked away under the shell.

"No," said the Captain again, "Painted Turtle doesn't bite, neither does Spotted Turtle," and from another pocket he pulled out a turtle of about the same size, only its black back was covered with bright yellow spots. "Neither does Muhlenburg's Turtle," he went on, taking out another turtle of about the same size, whose carapace was black with dim reddish blotches, while on each side of its head was a vivid orange patch. The Band applauded each new turtle enthusiastically.

"This one," said the Captain, "is a rare turtle and is named after the man who first discovered him."

Then he reached around to another pocket which was weighed down with something heavy. With some difficulty he pulled out a large turtle nearly eight inches long, with brick-red legs and neck. Its dull brown shell was marked with yellow and deeply carved into a series of high shields marked with fine grooves. The under-shell was yellow and red.

"This," said the Captain, "is the wood turtle, sometimes called the 'sculptured turtle.' When I found him he was close to the nest of an English pheasant in a big swamp, and if I hadn't caught him just in time would have eaten all her eggs. This turtle is good to eat," went on the Captain, "as I hope to prove to you at dinnertime."

Then he reached back and unbuttoned the largest pocket of all.

"Look out," said he, as he shook to the ground a big ugly turtle with a deeply grooved back and a long snaky head with a hooked beak. This turtle hissed fiercely and did not draw its head in as did the others, but opened its beak wide and snapped viciously at everything that came near.

"This gentle creature," said the Captain, "is Snapping Turtle and the only good thing about it is its taste. When cooked most people can't tell it from the diamond-backed terrapin except by the cost. This is a true turtle," he continued, "all the others which I have shown you are really terrapins. Once when I was a boy," he reminisced, "ninety or a hundred years ago, in the early spring my brother and I caught a big snapper which had crawled out of a pond into a little brook. We had to hoist it into a wheelbarrow to get it home and it weighed thirty-two pounds. In those days," he went on, "I had a collection of twenty-two spotted turtles."

There was still one pocket unexplored. It was Henny-Penny who put his hand in and pulled out a turtle whose shell was covered with bright yellow marks, many of them like the letter "E." The minute he came into the light Mr. Turtle drew his head and front feet into his shell and then clamped down a lid which was fastened to the upper end of his plastron with a hinge of muscle.

"He looks just like a box," said Henny-Penny, poking the shell cautiously.

"That's his name," said the Captain, "Box Turtle— the first inventor of the portable house. This one is Mr. Box Turtle because his eyes are red. Mrs. B. T. has yellow eyes."

"How did you find him?" inquired the Third.

"Well," said the Captain, "I met an old darky near the swamp where I was hunting and we got to talking snakes. He told me that he had seen that morning the track of a monstrous snake through the long grass. It was so heavy, he said, that it made a perfectly round path. I knew what that meant, so I went over to the place and followed the track and pretty soon, hidden in the grass, I found Mr. Box Turtle, who likes to make these paths where the grass is highest. He finds lots of insects there. Then, too, he is very fond of berries and in the blackberry season you will find his head and front feet all stained with berry juice. Mr. Box Turtle," continued the Captain, "is half way between the turtles, which live in the water, and the tortoises, which live entirely on land. He can swim, but he hates to do it, and if he falls into the water scrabbles along on the top like a floating buoy. Yet he has on his hind-feet traces of webs, so he is ranked with the turtles. Probably," lectured the Captain, "the split between the turtles and the tortoises begins with the Muhlenburg turtle, which has learned to eat out of water, something which other turtles, like the spotted and the painted turtles, can't do. Then comes the wood-turtle, which can swim perfectly, but prefers to live on land. Beyond the box turtle the real tortoises begin. They range from the gopher-tortoise, which digs so many burrows in the Southern States, up to the giant tortoise of the Galapagos Islands. One of them is in the New York Zoological Gardens and weighs three hundred and ten pounds, and is four feet long and over four hundred years old. I knew a boy once," went on the Captain, "who used to cut the initials 'G. W., 1776' on every box-turtle that he found, so if you come across a turtle with those initials, don't be too sure that you have found one of George Washington's pets."

"What are you going to do with this one?" inquired Trottie.

"I thought," answered the Captain, "that we might put him in the garden. He'll eat worms and insects, and a little lettuce once in a while. Then when winter comes on he will go underground and come back next spring, and if you children treat him well he will live here a good many years."

And that's how Boxy the Turtle came to live in the garden with Warty the Toad.

THE TREE TREASURE HUNT

The Captain came home one evening with a very mysterious look on his face. He at once called a meeting of the Band.

"Comrades," he said, shutting the door of the Den and looking carefully under the sofa and up the chimney, "I have just heard that there is a treasure hidden not many miles from here. All those in favor of a treasure hunt tomorrow will kindly make a noisy noise."

The vote was probably the finest collection of assorted sounds ever heard outside of a boiler factory. Right in the middle of it all, the door burst open and in rushed Mother, and Minnie the cook, and Annie the nurse, while at almost the same instant old John the gardener ran up on the porch with an axe, shouting, "Hould him! Hould him! I'm comin'!" under the impression that there was a fight on with some unusually ferocious robber.

The noise stopped suddenly and the Captain looked quite ashamed, as he explained that it was only the Band taking a vote.

Mother pretended to be very angry.

"Someday," she said, "you'll all be in terrible danger and you'll shout and yell and scream for help and not one of us will come. Will we, John?"

"Niver a step," called back John, as he clumped disappointedly down the steps, his unused axe over his shoulder.

The Band threw themselves on stern little Mother in a wave.

"You couldn't not come to your nice littly girl," besought Alice-Palace, while Trottie and the Third and Honey and Henny-Penny all tried to hug her at once.

"Well, perhaps not," relented Mother, "if you'll never make such disgusting noises again in the house."

The next afternoon found the Band in full marching order along old sunken Roberts Road, the beginning of so many of their adventures among the wild folk. Each one was armed with a bird sheet on which to check the names of all birds seen and heard, for the Captain had promised them field-glasses as soon as they could identify thirty different kinds of birds in a day. The Third and Trottie had won theirs, and the others were hard on their heels, all except Alice-Palace, who relied mostly on her imagination, much to the distress of her twin, the literal Henny-Penny.

As they marched in single file down the road, a slim little hawk with a buff, mottled waistcoat skimmed across a pasture from the top of a huge willow tree, hovered for a long moment over a patch of withered grass, and then darted off shrilling the slogan of his folk: "Kill-kill-kill-kill!"

"Sparrow hawk!" shouted the Captain and the Third.

"Sparrow hawk!" chorused Trottie and Honey a second later.

"Narrow hawk!" piped Alice.

"Not *narrow* hawk, *sparrow* hawk," objected Henny-Penny.

"No," said Alice firmly, "it's a *very* narrow hawk indeed and that's his name."

At Three Corners, where the little old yellow school-house stood, a flock of sleek buff birds with crests, a yellow band at the underside of their tails and a scowling black band above their eyes, flew out of a clump of highbush cranberries, wheeled all together like a military company and disappeared down the valley.

"Cedar birds," called out the bird experts. Around a bend in the road a flock of robins flew out of a tree.

"Apple tree birds," remarked Alice-Palace decisively, and no argument availed to change her decision. "They flewed out of an apple tree and that's their name," she maintained firmly.

Just before the Band reached old Tory Bridge, the Captain turned off into a bowl-shaped meadow. On three sides the green turf sloped down to a long level stretch covered with a thin growth of different trees with a thicket in their midst through which trickled a little stream. Near the fence stood a white-oak tree to which some ill-tempered owner had fastened a fierce sign which read, "Keep out. All trespassers are liable to be shot without notice." The cross owner had been gone many a long year, but the sign still stayed. It always gave the Band a delightful thrill to read it, and made them think of spring guns and mantraps.

At the edge of the grove the Captain halted them all.

"Comrades," he said in a whisper. "I have heard rumors that there is a clue to this Treasure hidden in the sign tree."

It was enough. With one accord the Band sprang upon that defenseless tree. Some searched among its gnarled roots. Others examined the lowest branches. It was Henny-Penny, however, who, boosted by Alice-Palace, fumbled back of the threatening old sign and drew out a crumpled slip of grimy paper. On the top had been laboriously inscribed in some red fluid, presumably blood, a skull and crossbones. Underneath in a very bad hand was written, "By the roots of the nearest black walnut tree. Captain Kidd." There was a moment's check. The Third, followed by all the others except Henny-Penny, ran to a nearby tree with close-knit bark and straight twigs. Henny-Penny regarded the tree doubtfully, and then searched the sky line until he found a tree which looked almost exactly like the other except that the upper twigs were twisted and crooked instead of straight. In a moment there was a shout and Henny-Penny waved over his head a crumpled piece of paper which said, "Go to the nearest tulip tree. Blackbeard the Pirate."

By the time the others had reached the place where Henny-Penny had dropped the paper, he had a good start toward a straight, slim tree with square-cut leaves, for he remembered that the Captain had once told the Band that the tulip tree was the only one in America which had square leaves, By its base was another message: "Look under the stone that stands between a spicebush and a white ash." This was a sticker. The Band had forgotten just how to tell spicebush. They ran sniffing the various nearby bushes like a pack of beagles. Finally it was Honey who found a bush whose crushed leaf smelled sweet and spicy and whose twigs broke as brittle as glass. Henny-Penny located the white ash, remembering again the difference between the white ash and the black walnut. The twigs of the white ash are blunt and point straight to the sky like fingers. It was not long before the combination was found, and the whole Band heaved up a big flat stone which stood there while the Third read off another message: "Look in the crotch of a dogwood tree. It will not bite, but you can tell it by its bark."

"I know," said Trottie, "its bark looks like the lizard-skin bag that Mother has, all covered with little square scales."

Sure enough, such a tree was soon found, filled with great white flowers, and in the crotch was another message, which said: "Look in the old red-eyed vireo's nest which hangs on a sour gum tree." This halted the whole Band. Not one of them remembered what a sour gum tree looked like, although the Third knew that it was the same as the tupelo and also the pepperidge. They scattered and searched the grove singly and in pairs.

It was Alice-Palace that found the next clue. She wasted no time in looking for trees sweet or sour. The year before she had learned the low hanging little woven white basket which the vireo makes for its nest, and she trotted hither and yon searching every low-swinging branch with her sharp eyes. Finally she came to a great tree with a deep corrugated bark whose upper limbs grew out at right angles from the trunk. On the tip of one of the lowest limbs she saw what she sought, a bleached and weather-beaten vireo's nest swinging in the wind. Pulling down the limb she found a precious folded paper, which contained the last message of all:

"I am buried. A red cedar, a black oak and a sassafras tree are equally distant from my grave.

(Signed)   "The Treasure."

Followed scamperings and scurryings and huntings galore. Everyone knew the red cedar tree with its dark green foliage. All the Band, too, knew the sassafras tree, because they were accustomed to nibble its leaves, some of which were trefoil and some single lobed, as well as the spicy bark of its twigs and the roots of its saplings. Only the Third knew the secret of the black oak. It had leaves whose tips were pointed, but so were those of the red oak, scarlet oak and the pin oak. He located a tree with a black bark not far from a cedar tree. Opening his trusty jackknife he whittled through the outer bark. The inside bark was a deep saffron-yellow, the hallmark of the black oak. By this time the rest of the children had found a sassafras tree and the red cedar. The sassafras and the black oak stood at the points of the triangle. The

Third paced off five paces from each tree and where the lines came together the whole Band commenced to dig, some with jackknives, some with crooked sticks. A foot below the soft mold some one's knife clinked against metal. Alice-Palace threw herself headlong into the hole and scrabbled out with the treasure, a great tin box, which held exactly two pounds of assorted chocolates.

An hour later the Band, sticky but satisfied, started homeward.

"The trouble about treasures is that they don't last," sighed Honey.

"Well," said the Captain, "there are ten trees and shrubs which you will always remember. That's a treasure that will last."

BLINDIE THE MOLE

It was Henny-Penny who first made the acquaintance of Blindie. He was trotting down a slope of the lawn, very busy in visiting all of the trees and bugs and flowers which he had not seen since yesterday. Down by the Violet Hill, where the first violets come in the spring, he stopped to look at the Perplexing Trees which grew on that slope. There were four of them and they always bothered him. One was a spruce, one was a pine, one was a hemlock, and the other was a balsam fir. Every time the Band walked past there with the Captain they had to pass an examination on these trees. So today Henny-Penny was saying over to himself, "Short needles, hemlock; long needles, pine; middle-sized needles all round the stem, spruce; middle-sized needles flat on one side with nice smell, fir." Just as he said the word "fir" right at his feet there was an earthquake. At any rate, where the ground was covered with pine needles close to the trees, the earth moved and broke and rose up in little waves and dropped

down again, leaving a long, hollow ridge. If that wasn't
an earthquake, Henny-Penny didn't know what it was.

At first he was going to run, for he had always heard
that earthquakes were dangerous. As nothing seemed to
happen, however, he stuck the toe of his stumpy little
shoe into the very middle of the earthquake. It struck
something round and fuzzy, and he kicked out upon the
pine needles a strange little animal covered with soft,
fine black fur. It had a long, flexible snout, but no eyes
or ears. Its forepaws were broad and flat, with sharp,
curved claws and white wrinkled palms, and were bowed
out so that when brought together the backs touched
each other. The minute this strange animal touched
the ground it began to swim right down through the
earth before Henny-Penny's astonished eyes. As it was
going out of sight he pulled it up just in time. Holding
it carefully by the back of the neck, so that it couldn't
bite, Henny-Penny started for the house. On the way he
passed the big lilac bush, by which stood the sand box,
where he and Alice-Palace, his twin, built tremendous
forts and laid long lines of railways and planned other
important building and mining operations. A bright
idea came to him. He would put Blindie, as he had already named the little beastie, on the sand and let him
dig as many tunnels as he pleased, for underneath and
on all sides was an inch-thick plank. He did so, and
with one stroke Mr. Blindie swam out of sight. That
evening, when the Captain came home, he was met
by the Band, who all together and at once told him of
the day's discovery.

"Quite so," remarked the Captain, when they at last stopped for breath; "I understand the whole thing. Henny-Penny's caught a Blindie. He's not lost, only you can't find him. Come along and we'll mine for him in the sandbox."

So they went out with a lantern and a spade, and after a lot of free-hand digging the Captain found Blindie in a tunnel in one corner of the box.

"Fellow citizens," he began, impressively, taking a firm grip on Blindie's plush-like fur, "this fierce and enormous quadruped which I hold so bravely in my right hand is known as the Mole. He's called Mole because that's his name."

"We'd rather call him Blindie," interrupted Alice-Palace at this point.

"Quite right," said the Captain, "that's a better name; but in order that ignorant persons may entirely understand you, just add the word 'Mole' to it and call him 'Blindie the Mole.' There are three kinds of blindies in our part of the United States," he went on. "One is called the star-nosed mole because, instead of having a pointed nose like Honey-Bee, or a snub nose like Henny-Penny, or a very beautiful nose like the ones Alice-Palace and I have, he prefers a nose with a star at the end of it, for its snout ends like a flat disk covered with tiny points or fingers. The star-nosed mole," went on the Captain, "is only found in wet, swampy ground. This blindie here," he continued, "is the common or naked-tailed mole, which has a short bare tail. Then there is another rarer mole called the hairy-tailed mole, which has a hairy tail. Sometimes," finished the Captain, "the shrew, which has a long snout, too, is taken for the mole. It is only about half the size and doesn't have flat, spadelike forepaws. When Blindie is at home he lives from twelve to fifteen inches below the ground, deep enough to escape any plow."

"But, Fathy," objected Henny-Penny, "this one was only an inch or so underground when I caught him."

"He was in one of his hunting tunnels," explained the Captain. "Every mole has a lot of shallow runways just under the top of the ground. He goes through all of these every day and picks up earthworms and grubs and any other insect which he may find there. When game gets scarce, he digs new tunnels and he always takes great care of them. If you make a hole in any of the little ridges which you see along the lawn and go there the next day, you will find that Mr. Mole has mended it. His nest is a little round room four or five inches across and about a foot underground, and filled with fine grass which he has pulled in by the roots from below."

"Does he go to sleep in the winter like the chipmunk and the woodchuck?" inquired Trottie.

"No," said the Captain, "the mole stays awake all winter. When it gets cold he goes down deep below the frost and hunts as he does in summer through his tunnels, only, of course, they are very much deeper."

"John the gardener says," interrupted the Third, "that moles do lots of harm and that we ought to kill this one."

There was a loud wail of protest from Henny-Penny and Alice-Palace, and it was some time before the Captain could be heard.

"They do some harm," he explained, "but they do more good, so we won't kill any blindies on this place. They don't eat roots or plants, although sometimes different kinds of mice which use their tunnels do and Mr. Mole gets the blame. They do make trouble in gardens and on lawns by displacing the seeds and roots and making long ugly ridges. On the other hand, a mole eats its own weight every day in white grubs, earthworms, beetles, larvae, spiders, centipedes and other insects, many of which do harm to plants. Besides killing off the grubs, moles help the gardeners in another way. Their tunnels mix the soil and sift the earth so that the air and water can get in and, in the long run, plants grow a great deal better after a mole has been around, although he may disturb their roots a good deal at first."

"Brownie, John's fox terrier," said Honey, "smelled of Blindie and we were afraid he was going to bite him, but he only squivveled up his nose and went away."

"Yes," replied the Captain, "there are not many animals that will touch a mole. Their fur has a curious smell which dogs and cats don't like, and hardly any of them are ever caught either by hawks or owls. Heavy rainstorms and floods are about the only things that Blindie fears, because then the water may fill his tunnels and drown him."

"And now, comrades," concluded the Captain, "since you have heard the whole of this interesting and instructive lecture, let's take Blindie back home."

"But we want him for a pet," objected all the Band.

"Yes," said the Captain, "but what does Blindie want? He ought to have something to say about this. Do you think it's fair to take a little animal and shut him up in a cage just because you want to look at him? Good sportsmen don't keep wild things in cages."

The next morning a procession might have been seen marching down Violet Hill. It was made up of the members of the Band with Henny-Penny carrying Blindie again. When they reached the hunting-tunnel where the earthquake had been, each one smoothed his soft, plushy fur for the last time and then Henny-Penny set him gently down on the outside of one of the ridges. He never even hesitated. With one plunge of his powerful paws he swam down through the pine needles. There was a little pattering sound underground and Blindie was at home again.

A CHRISTMAS ANGEL

The nights are too long," complained Henny-Penny as he got up for the fifth time the night before Christmas, only to find that it was three A. M.

"How many days before next Christmas?" inquired the pessimistic Alice-Palace from her crib, feeling that the Day was already far spent.

At last and at last the sun peeped up over the edge of Violet Hill. At the very first gleam the Band arose with a whoop. Down from the third story trooped the Third and Trottie and Honey, while the twins, Henny-Penny and Alice-Palace, by a flank movement, joined them at the foot of the staircase. Waiting a moment to form ranks they all burst into the Captain's room with a shout of "Merry Christmas" that nearly brought the plaster down. Over the fireplace hung a tremendous gray plaid shawl which a Scotch lord had once given to the Captain's grandfather in the days when men wore shawls instead of overcoats. For two generations it had been hung over fireplaces to cover up Christmas stockings. Underneath, for each member of the Band, there was a big stocking and a little stocking, both of them very lumpy and knobby and crammed to bursting with different presents. Each member of the Band rushed back to bed with the little stocking, while the big stocking and the presents too large for any stocking were kept until after breakfast.

Immediately sounded loud squeals and other assorted noises from the little-ups while the grown-ups tried vainly to sleep again before the rising bell. Then came a wonderful Christmas breakfast, and the story of the first Christmas, and the taking down of the rest of the stockings and the trying out of all the presents, and more squeals, and greetings from other grown-ups and little-ups who had flocked in to compare presents. So it was after ten when the Band finally started out for their annual Christmas bird walk. Every holiday they had a bird walk and kept a list of all the birds seen and heard, the which was noted down in the "Band Book," a big leather-covered volume in which the Captain inscribed and recorded the doings of the Band year by year.

It was a dark day and the white snow crunched under foot in the stinging cold. Straight for Fox Valley the Band headed, following the little winding fox path which led through the marsh and down between two round, green hills and across the brook through the beech woods, and ended at Blacksnake Den. As they crunched along in the snow, overhead through the gray air passed a little flock of greenish birds with white wing bars, which dipped up and down as they flew, while down through the air came a faint, sweet, canary like note.

"Goldfinches!" shouted Trottie and the Third together.

"They don't look very goldy," objected Alice-Palace.

"You see," explained the Captain, "they're wearing their winter suits. Mr. Goldfinch has put away his best black cap and yellow coat with black sleeves because, of course, they would wear out if he wore them all the year around. He always keeps the two white bars on his wings though," finished the Captain.

As they marched in single file, suddenly a little piece of bark on the side of a white oak tree seemed to move, and before their very eyes began to circle the trunk and go up in a spiral path. Through their field glasses they saw that it was a little brown and gray bird with a long curved beak, and the Captain told them that it was the brown creeper, who always goes up a tree in tiny little hops in a spiral and has to fly down. Then the Captain told them how for a long while no one could ever find the nest of a brown creeper, until at last it was found under strips of bark on dead trees.

Down in the marsh the path led past a swamp maple. In the fork of a bare branch was a round nest all silver-gray and woven out of strips of the pods and floss of the milkweed. Trottie climbed up and brought it down for the Band's collection of nests. When looked at closely it seemed to have two stories. The Captain poked his finger down through the bottom of the first, and there underneath was another nest with two eggs, one pale bluish-white and the other speckled all over with cinnamon-brown. Then the Captain told them the story of that nest. It was made by Mrs. Goldfinch. After she had laid her first egg along had come Mrs. Cowbird, who never builds a nest of her own but always puts her eggs into other birds' nests. There they hatch first and the little cowbird crowds out or starves to death all the other birds in the nest. When Mrs. Goldfinch found what had happened she told Mr. Goldfinch, and they had gone to work and built another nest right over the ugly, fatal egg.

At the edge of the swamp they heard a loud whistle, and suddenly blood-red against the white snow flashed out a crested, brilliant cardinal grosbeak. The Captain had them all stand still, and then he gave the adventure call of the Band—the loud whistled note of the cardinal. For a minute the bird seemed to listen, and then suddenly dived into the thicket and whistled back even louder and much clearer than the Captain could.

"Oh, the nice, dear cunningsome!" exclaimed Alice-Palace as they listened to the bird and the Captain calling each other. "I wisht I could take him home."

"He is happier out in the woods," said the Captain, "than he could be in a cage."

All through the beech woods were little flocks of slate colored snow birds and blue jays. Just before they came to Blacksnake Den they heard a curious grunting note, and a gray bird with white cheeks and a white breast ran up and down a tree ahead of them grunting to itself, "Yank, yank, yank." Suddenly as they watched him he stopped and broke out into a loud "Quee, quee, quee, quee," all in one tone. The Captain told them that this was the spring song of the white-breasted nuthatch, and that he had never heard one sing so early in the winter.

"I guess," said Trottie, "that it's a Christmas carol for us."

On their way back through Fern Valley they had a glimpse of a bird with a long beak, black cravat, gold-lined wings, and a white patch over the tail. It was Mr. Flicker, who had decided to winter north instead of south for a change.

The last bird of all came late that night. The Band had been tucked away, tired out after a happy and exciting day. The Captain was dozing in front of the fire over a Christmas book. Suddenly from Henny-Penny's room came an S.O.S.

"Fathy!" he shouted, "come quick, there's a nangel in my room. I can hear him flappin' around. Hurry!"

The Captain hurried, for angels rarely appeared on any of his bird lists. By the time he reached the room and turned on the light Henny-Penny had burrowed for safety so deep under the bedclothes that it was a wonder he ever came to the surface again. At first the Captain could see nothing, and told Mother, who had come in, that he was afraid that the angel must have escaped out of the open window. Just then he turned around, and there it was perched on the picture moulding. It was a little reddish-brown screech owl with round yellow eyes and tufted ears and a funny hooked beak. The Captain tried to steal up behind him, but without moving his position the little head with the yellow eyes turned around and around and followed the Captain as if set on a double joint. As the Captain came close, suddenly there sounded a sharp, rattling, clicking noise.

"Oo," bellowed Henny-Penny from beneath the bedclothes, "is the nangel breakin' your bones, Fathy?"

However, it was nothing but the little owl snapping his beak, the favorite owl trick to drive away visitors. With a quick jump the Captain caught him. At first Mr. Screech Owl puffed up and clicked his beak and pretended to be very fierce, but when the Captain stroked his fluffy back he snuggled down into his hand and seemed to like it. The Captain woke up all the Band and showed them the last bird of the day, and then with some difficulty persuaded the little owl to fly out of the window into the cold night.

Henny-Penny was much relieved to find out his mistake.

"Cuddly little owls are better'n big old nangels," he said.

Colophon

Nathaniel Hartsough, Gabriela Siwiec and Samantha Wyld, editing interns at Stockton University during spring 2018, edited this volume. Tom Kinsella and Paul W. Schopp supervised the publication.

The text is set in 12 point Adobe Caslon Pro. Pagination does not follow the original edition. Gary Schenck designed the cover.

❧

The mission of the South Jersey Culture & History Center is to help foster awareness within local communities of the rich cultural and historical heritage of southern New Jersey, to promote the study of this heritage, especially among area students, and to produce publishable materials that provide lasting and deepened understanding of this heritage.